# TORFAEN HEROES

## of

# WORLD WAR TWO

ISBN 0 9520543 8 8

Published by W.G. Lloyd, Cwmbran, and printed by
J & P Davison, 3 James Place, Treforest, Pontypridd CF37 1SQ

# TORFAEN HEROES
## of
# WORLD WAR TWO

by

W.G. Lloyd

Printed by
J & P Davison, 3 James Place, Treforest, Pontypridd.

# INTRODUCTION

This was not an easy book to write simply because none of the participants wanted to talk of their inspiring achievements. Slowly the facts began to emerge, mostly from other sources, and piece-by-piece the human stories of the modest heroes were retrieved before being lost in the relentless march into history.

Each account never failed to astound me, and it soon became apparent that I have been privileged to record the following unique events.

Let us not waste the wondrous gift of freedom these brave people have given us.

W.G. Lloyd, August 2003.

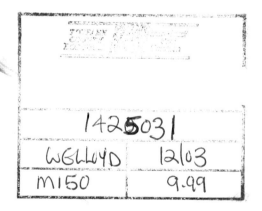

# ACKNOWLEDGEMENT

I wish to thank the following for their kindness and positive help: Staff of the Gwent Record Office, staff of the National Library of Wales, staff of the Cardiff Local Studies Library, staff of the Newport Local Studies Library, staff of the Cwmbran Local Studies Library, staff of the Public Record Office, London, staff of the National Army Museum, staff of the Imperial War Museum and all those who provided documents, photographs and memories of their loved ones.

Sylvia Adey
Chris Appleby
Gillian Attwood
Philip Attwood
Lyn Badham
Howard Bailey
Johanne Bailey
Neil Bailey
Keith Barrell
Frank Beacham
Denys Benham
Megan Benham
Darrel Booth
Gaynor Booth
Ralph Booth
Stella Bradley
Michael Bradshaw
Brian Cater
Philip Cater
Rita Charles
Jennifer Clarke
Steve Cunningham
Ron Davies
Beryl Dibben
Dorset Echo
John England
Mavis Drew
Tony Drew
John Duffield
Peggy May Duffield
Isobel Edwards
Adrian Rowe-Evans
Robert Everett

Peter Gallagher
Albert E. Gauntlett
Cornelias Harris
Doreen Harris
Shirley Horler
Keith Jackson
Ivor Jarvis
Barbara Jones
Phyllis Jones
Terry I. Jones
Robert Kerr
R.H. Knight
Jack Lewis
Jacqueline Lias
Raymonde Lias
Allison Lloyd
Eva Lloyd
Malcolm McCann
Margot Maxwell
Jennie Meredith
Rev. B.J. Morgan
Janet Morgan
Jennifer Morgan
Mair Morgan
Margaret Morgan
Margaret S. Murgatroyd
Walter D. Murgatroyd
Edward Niblett
Mary Niblett
David Nicholas
Roger Nolan
Colin D. Nunnerley
Joan Pelopida

Ian Pritchard
K.D. Roderick
Maureen Roberts
Eleanor Thomas
Sandra Seabourne
Colin Smith
Susan Smith
William Hina Smith
Barbara Strange
Len Strange
John Thomson
Pauline Thomson
Duncan Lloyd Turner
Joan Lloyd Turner
Bill Wadley
Morgan Waters
Margaret Watkins
Ron Webb
Muriel Wheatstone
W.G. Wheatstone
Jack Wheeler
Mary Wilcox
Frank Williams
Huw P. Williams
Peggy Williams
Robert Williams
Ann Wills

# JOHN APPLEBY
## Distinguished Flying Medal and Polish Cross of Valour

Born July 29 1922, the third son of John and Annie Louisa Appleby, of Woodland Street, Cwmbran. John Appleby would have a number of remarkable experiences during World War Two. Educated at St. Dial's and West Monmouthshire School, he became an ironworker before enlisting in the 4th Battalion, The Monmouthshire Regiment, on 1st September 1939. His miss-statement regarding his young age was soon discovered resulting in his discharge from the colours on the 19 February 1940.

As soon as he became of age John re-enlisted in September 1941, but his choice of service had changed to the Royal Air Force Volunteer Reserve. By 1944, he was a Flight Sergeant attached to 267 Squadron. With this squadron John participated in a number of special missions, one of which won him the Polish Cross of Valour. As an important member of a team he took part in the dramatic rescue of the Polish leader Thomasz Arciszewski, who was picked up from an airstrip in German-occupied Poland.

In August 1944, John arrived home for ten days special leave during which time he received the Polish Cross of Valour at the Polish Embassy, London, and was afterwards the guest of the Embassy at a lavish banquet. The award was discussed at a meeting of the Cwmbran Council and a letter of congratulation forwarded to his parent's home. This was followed a few months later by the award of the Distinguished Flying Medal. The citation reads:

> 'He completed numerous operations against the enemy, in the course of which he has invariably displayed the utmost fortitude, courage and devotion to duty.'

Jack, as his friends knew him, never married. He lived the remainder of his life in Cwmbran while employed as a quality controller at Girlings Ltd. In his younger days he enjoyed the game of rugby and spent many happy hours singing tenor in the Trenewydd Singers. In later years his passion was gardening, tending his nearby allotment on a daily basis until too ill to continue. Very much esteemed, he died on the 19 February 1996.

# DENNIS ARTHUR ATTWOOD
## Military Medal

Born June 6, 1920, at Newport. He attended Durham Road School with his brother and two sisters. Several years before the outbreak of World War Two, Reginald Attwood moved his family to The Gables, Park Road, Pontypool, and became a well-known fruiterer in the small town. Dennis worked for his father after leaving school and at a young age his sporting attributes began to show when he played cricket for Pontypool Park Cricket Club.

He enlisted in 1939 and served throughout the Second World War. Going overseas in August 1941, he took part in the fighting at Tobruk, and left just a few hours before the Germans entered the town. Later, in 1944, 329756 Lance Corporal Dennis Arthur Attwood, 3rd Kings Own Hussars, Royal Armoured Corps, was awarded an immediate Military Medal for rescue and first aid work in Italy. The action for which he was commended states:

> 'At Galese on 19 June 1944 Trooper Attwood was driving a 15cwt Armed Medical Scout Car which was sent off to bring in a badly wounded man. In order to reach this man he had to drive one mile down a stretch of road which was under direct enemy observation and which was being very heavily shelled and mortared. Three quarters of the way down this road he was brought to a full stop by a bridge which had just been destroyed by enemy shell fire. Nothing daunted, he and his orderly dismounted, crossed the broken bridge and walked the remaining 500 yards. They collected the wounded man, carried him back to the vehicle and brought him safely in. In Citta Della Pieve on 17 June 1944 he again distinguished himself by driving his vehicle twice into the outskirts of the village to collect wounded tank crews and infantry men. On each occasion the whole area was being heavily shelled and mortared and snipers were operating from nearby houses. His coolness and courage under these difficult circumstances was an example to all who saw him.'

After the war Dennis returned safely home and continued to assist his father. He would later take over the successful business. In 1949, he married Marion

Turner, the daughter of a Pontypool businessman. They had two sons Arthur and Phillip.

During the war Dennis became a friend of Tom Finney, the legendary England football international, and played with the great man until his own skills reached a high standard. They would remain close friends all through their lives. Throughout the eastern valley the young man became a well-known and popular sportsman. He was a member of a number of local cup winning football teams and captain of Pontnewynydd Cricket Club for two years. A further long spell with Panteg Cricket Club eventually resulted in him becoming President of the prestigious club.

This brave and likable man passed away on July 15, 2002.

# GEOFFREY BAILEY
## Distinguished Service Medal

Geoffrey Bailey was born in a district which produced an amazing number of heroes. Aptly named Freeholdland, Pontnewynydd, he entered the world on December 29, 1920, the youngest of three boys belonging to Mr and Mrs Wilfred Bailey. While his father worked at a nearby colliery, Geoffrey attended the local school with his two brothers and four sisters. Leaving school at fifteen years of age the young man worked for a while in an office at the head of a colliery.

When old enough Geoffrey enlisted in the Royal Navy and was immediately sent to the training ship *H.M.S. Impregnable*. His first ship was *H.M.S. Royal Oak*, on which he served until just short of his nineteenth birthday. In July 1939, Able Seaman Bailey left the *Royal Oak* for *H.M.S. Hardy*. Fate had been kind to the young Pontnewynydd man for the British battleship *H.M.S. Royal Oak* was torpedoed at anchor in Scapa Flow just over a month later with the loss of 810 men.

In April 1940, came the first large engagement of the war up until that time with the First Battle of Narvik. A destroyer flotilla went out, the *Hardy* among it, and courageously attacked a far superior German naval force off Narvik, Norway. A snowstorm raged that day as Captain Warburton-Lee, from Wales, led the five destroyers, his mission was to prevent German occupation of Norway's ice-free port. The German U-boats and destroyers guarding Narvik were taken by surprise. Warburton Lee opened fire, sinking and damaging three destroyers and six merchant ships. Suddenly from a neighbouring fiord, five previously unseen German destroyers emerged, their guns blazing at the British intruders, sinking or damaging four of the Royal Navy attackers. Badly wounded on the bridge, Captain Warbuton-Lee died shortly after while being taken to the shore. The first Victoria Cross of the war was awarded posthumously to him for his gallantry in the attack.

A number of Eastern Valley men were present at the battle with some of them sadly losing their lives. Able Seaman Geoffrey Bailey, D/JX. 151861, survived the

ferocious encounter that day and was awarded the Distinguished Service Medal
for his courage. In his unpublished biography he wrote:

'*April 7th. – Half way across our skipper Warbuton-Lee ordered the whole
crew, except those on watch, to muster on the seamen's mess deck forward
and there we were told where we were bound for. German ore ships had
been travelling to and from Narvik carrying the precious ore to Germany
under the eyes of the Royal Navy, who were powerless to stop them because
they were inside Norwegian Territorial Waters thereby violating
international law, not that it worried the Germans.*

*April 10th. – ...3.15 am, the snow had cleared and it was getting light,
we could now see where we were, the fiord at this point was very wide and
we increased speed a little bit, I didn't see any sign of life on the shore...The
fiord widened into a sort of bay. Like a hunter approaching the lion's den,
we crept warily forward to what was obviously the entrance to the harbour.
Our faces set, the gunlayer with his eyes on the gunsights, AB Hay ready
to shove a round into the breach, the two loading numbers standing by with
the second round in their arms, and myself with my eyes glued to the range
dial, my ears cocked to catch the slightest order from the bridge. We were
ready for heaven knows what, the whole German fleet for all we knew...We
swung gentle to port and nosed our way into the harbour, it was full of ships
flying the Swastika. I saw a small sailing boat with a couple of people in it,
I felt like shouting to them to scram before they got hurt. I looked through
the gun port...and lying between them was a German destroyer making a
beautiful target for our torpedoes...I heard the swish of the D.C. tinfish as
it left the tube, for a second I saw its wake and then a terrific roar as the
German destroyer blew up. She had been hit in the magazine, pieces blew
hundreds of feet in the air and then we opened up with our guns. It was like
hell let loose.*

*We blazed away with everything we had; we fired torpedoes at every
likely target. Guns on the Nazi merchant ships opened fire, but it was
ineffective and we didn't have a scratch. We concentrated our fire on two
more destroyers lying at anchor. We scored several hits by this time. We
had turned around until we faced the mouth of the harbour with our
accompanying destroyers coming up astern. We came out of the harbour
and swung around and slowed down for a breather and were told to stand
by for the next run. We were in high spirits, not one of our ships had a
scratch. When the last of our ships came out, we increased speed and with
guns blazing went back into the harbour, which by now looked to me like a
harbour of sinking ships. We turned our fire on the shore batteries.
Keeping close in shore we pumped round after round into the gun nests up
on the mountainside. They fired back, but with no results, as we were too*

5

close inland for their guns to bear on us. We couldn't see the guns but we were firing at the flashes, which seemed to be effective, anyhow, the firing by them became spasmodic. No. 2 Gun turned its fire on a howitzer on the foreshore, which was worrying us. A few rounds finished that one off. We fired on the remaining merchant ships as we came around and scored hits on them and then came out of the harbour a second and last time, as we thought, but we found we still had a few tinfish D.C. left so in we went again and fired these at the pier and jetty, at the same time narrowly missing being hit by one ourselves fired by one of their crippled destroyers, it passed underneath us. By now the harbour was in chaos and when we came out there was hardly anything in the harbour, which hadn't either been sunk or badly damaged by shell or torpedoes and we felt quite proud of ourselves, but not for long!

As we came out of the harbour for the last time we saw two grey ships approaching head-on at full speed. We thought it was more help, as though we had needed it. We were mistaken; it was help alright, for the enemy in the shape of two destroyers heavily armed. "Enemy bearing right ahead" I bellowed, I almost lost my tonsils doing so. Our guns were still pointing towards the harbour and we lost precious seconds in bringing them to bear on the enemy. Jock looked around the gunshield as the enemy came at us at full speed. "Now we are for it" he murmured "Your telling me" I replied as he slewed around on his gunlayer's seat and gripped his gunlayer's handles and stared at his pointer intently. Looking at him gave me confidence. All of this was happening in seconds and then came the enemy's first salvo CRACK! CRACK! They landed either side of us sending spray high into the air and then we fired our guns. The enemy's second salvo came over. I saw a flash, felt the ship shudder. I didn't realise at the time we had been hit, I heard someone scream. I gripped my range dial wheels more tightly to prevent myself from screaming, our loading was great. Everyone kept shouting and praying, "Please God help us." "Get that ammunition up here" was the last words he ever uttered, there was a great roar, and a blinding flash and I was flung up against the gunshield and felt a burning sensation on my face. I put my hand to my face and felt warm blood coursing down it. I pulled myself erect and then noticed my hand was shattered. I wanted to faint, but couldn't. I looked around; everything seemed to be on fire, the deck was in shambles. Jock was lying on the deck. I recognised him by his coat, his head had been blown off. Lying up against the guardrails was AB Hay with a terrible wound in his head. The captain of the gun lay sprawled on his side, his face a mass of blood. Where were the others, had they all been killed? I got down on the gundeck. A German destroyer passed at that moment firing like hell. Shells were thudding into the ship's side, screaming overhead, it was hell with a vengeance.

*I was not alone on the gundeck as I thought for the trainer came around the gun and asked me if I was alright. I nodded my head. He grimaced "That's a bad un" he murmured. I looked down on the upper deck; men were struggling to get the boats out. We were going down very slowly I noticed and we were near the shore. I heard someone shout, "Abandon ship." I clambered down on to the upper deck and caught a fleeting glimpse of our trainer jumping overboard. With the help of a seaman I got my coat and oilskin off. I got into a boat, which was lowered into the water. We started to push the boat away from the ship's side, but the inevitable happened, the boat being overloaded capsized, and I was flung into the water. I went under and came up gasping for breath. I grabbed the keel of the boat, but a couple of other blokes had the same idea and the boat went under again. I gave it up and started to swim for it on my back. I had swum 20 yards when I heard someone shouting to me to stand up. I stood up; the water came up to my knees. I had been swimming like hell in two feet of water? All this time the Germans were firing at us and when I looked back I saw five destroyers circling around taking pot shots at us. It was great fun for them.*

*We walked for what seemed like hundreds of miles when eventually we reached a house. I walked into the house and was racked with pain, trembling with chattering teeth and shaking limbs. I was freezing cold. The boys ripped curtains off the windows and grabbed any kind of clothing, undressed and put them on until the house looked like the backstage of a pantomime.'*

Able Seaman Bailey, half frozen with cold, and with most of his hand blown away, sat in the house for one-and-a-half hours and never murmured. The local people immediately got the survivors to safety and the injured young seaman to a safe hospital. Here, the remainder of his hand was amputated. For a while he was posted as missing in action. It was several weeks later that his anxious father received notification that his son was off the danger list and on his way home. While convalescing in an English hospital the 19-year-old seaman received numerous letters. One he would particularly treasure was from the widow of his skipper, Mrs Warbuton Lee.

Invalided out of the Royal Navy, Geoffrey Bailey D.S.M., was deservedly feted when he arrived home. At a specially prepared presentation evening the young man received an inscribed gold watch and War Loan Bonds from the people of the district. From the staff and scholars of his old school he gratefully accepted a silver cigarette case. His indomitable spirit soon began to surface and he commenced an evening commercial course at Abersychan Technical Institute. He immediately became a popular student and the staff were particularly keen to give him a good start in his new walk of life.

By September 1941, Goff, as he liked to be known, was fully recovered and attended an investiture at Buckingham Palace where King George VI pinned the Distinguished Service Medal on his chest. The King chatted to his son and as his proud father looked on he would say, "I shall never forget this moment for as long as I live."

As the war progressed Goff settled into employment at the Royal Ordnance Factory, Glascoed, and did well. It would not be long before he met a delightful young lady. In December 1942, he married Miss Doreen Meredith, the only child of Mr and Mrs T. Meredith, of Coed Wood, Blaenavon. The wedding took place at St. Peter's Church, Blaenavon, and they had two sons, Brian and Christopher.

While living in Blaenavon, Geoff, worked at R.O.F. Glascoed for nineteen years and having been successful in a civil service examination, he transferred to the Ministry of Social Security. He later received promotion to the position of executive officer.

For many years the Narvik hero served the Blaenavon people well. He was chairman of the British Legion, treasurer of the local Labour Party, chairman of the governing body of Blaenavon Secondary School, chairman of the Council, and was appointed a magistrate in 1966. He considered it a great honour to become Mayor of Blaenavon. What little leisure time he had was spent following sport and enjoying a game of bowls.

This fine man died June 28, 1972. A sympathy card from the surviving members of H.M.S Hardy reads: *To the family of our shipmate and comrade, Geoffrey Bailey, a brave man at Narvik, 10th April 1940. We will remember him.*

# WILFRED BAILEY
## Distinguished Service Medal

Wilfred Bailey, born January 21, 1909, at Freeholdland, Pontnewynydd, Torfaen, the son of a colliery engine driver and one of three serving brothers. He attended the local school and worked as a collier for several years before joining the Royal Navy in 1925. He would serve with distinction until 1947.

During his career he served on thirty-one different ships, was in Malta for the period the island received its heaviest bombing, and survived his ships being sunk on two occasions. After one sinking he was in the water for twenty-four hours before rescued. It was while serving on the destroyer HMS *Lively* that he was awarded the Distinguished Service Medal for gallantry during a Mediterranean action. The destroyer was lost in action and although injured in the water, Petty Officer Bailey soon received assistance. Unfortunately, the rescue ship was bombed and the force of the explosion threw him back into the water, where he remained for four hours until picked up a second time. Evacuated immediately to hospital, he luckily had not been seriously injured.

While on leave Wilf married Iris Shelley, of Corporation Road, Newport. The wedding took place in St. John's Church, Maindee, Newport and they had three sons, Clive, Howard and Neil. After discharge Wilf worked for many years as an electrician at the Royal Ordnance Factory, Caerwent. He enjoyed his retirement and had by this time become an accomplished snooker player. This brave man of the sea died on March 13, 1983.

# THOMAS LEONARD BAKER
**Military Medal**

The son of Mr and Mrs William Baker, Bridge Cottage, Blaenavon, Monmouthshire. After attending the local school Tom Baker was employed for some time at Blaenavon Company's Big Pit Colliery. When reaching the correct age, he immediately joined the Northamptonshire Regiment and was a member of the British Expeditionary Force at the outbreak of World War Two. He was in the evacuation from Dunkirk and later served in North Africa. It was while in this campaign that the young Blaenavon man's name appeared in the June 11, 1943 issue of the *London Gazette*. For gallant and distinguished service No. 4032842 Thomas Leonard Baker, Northamptonshire Regiment, had been awarded the Military Medal. The account of the action for which he was commended states:

> '*Corporal Baker was in command of Stretcher Bearers of "C" Coy, 5 Northamptons, who on the morning of 8 April 43, were ordered to attack a position on Hill AE DEREJ 473373, which was on the right flank of the battalion attack.*
>
> *"C" Coy captured and occupied the position under heavy mortar and machine gun fire and suffered heavy casualties.*
>
> *The Stretcher Bearers under Corporal Baker at once commenced to evacuate the wounded back to the Medjez Road, a distance of about two miles, over exceedingly difficult country and under heavy fire from flak. Corporal Baker made this gruelling journey ten times under fire with his men during the day, encouraging them to further efforts.*
>
> *By his action 18 wounded men were evacuated and four lives definitely saved.*
>
> *At all times he has shown great personal courage, coolness and valour and by his personal efforts and disregard to danger is an example to all.*'

After the war Tom Baker married and later lived in Newport, Monmouthshire.

# DAVID RICHARD JAMES BARRELL
## Distinguished Flying Medal

Born in 1914, Dave Barrell would later take part in many operational flights over enemy territory during the dark days of World War Two. The son of Mr A.G. Barrel, of 13 College Road, Penygarn, Pontypool, a well-known station master at Abergavenny and Pontypool Road Railway Stations, he first joined the army, but came out and later joined the Royal Air Force.

Flight Sergeant Barrell took part in European and Middle East operational flying from 1940 until the end of the war. His role as wireless operator would be a crucial one on numerous occasions. During one such flight, the Lancaster he was flying in became badly shot up and although seriously wounded in the foot, Flight Sergeant Barrell played a big part in helping the aircraft to return to base. For his courage David Barrell received the Distinguished Flying Medal. His citation states:

> *'Flight Sergeant Barrell has taken part in operational flights since October 1940 and has served in the European and Middle East theatres of war. Throughout this long period he has consistently shown the greatest ability and keenness in performing his duties as a wireless operator.'*

He was later promoted to Warrant Officer. When the war ended he also held the Air Efficiency Award, the 1939 Star, the Air Crew Europe Star, the Africa Star, the Burma Star, the Defence Medal and the Victory Medal.

After the war Dave Barrell tried to settle back into civilian life, but appears to have missed the routine of the Royal Air Force. He rejoined in 1952 and accepted a drop in rank to corporal. He was finally discharged in 1960 and went to work for Sterling Metals, Nuneaton. His children number three sons and one daughter.

Dave died suddenly in 1961, at the young age of forty-seven years, and was given a military funeral. As his coffin, covered by the Union Jack, was taken into St. Mary's Church, representatives of the Royal Air Force and members of Nuneaton Air Training Corps lined the path. The moving event was filmed and shown in cinemas around the country.

# STANLEY BATEMAN
### Distinguished Service Medal

Fred Bateman, of 41 Rose Cottage, Pontnewynydd, had been toughened by years of work as a collier and this seemed to reflect in his youngest son. Stanley Bateman, born 1920, at Pontnewynydd, became the younger of two boys with three sisters. After receiving his education at Snatchwood School he worked at Pontnewynydd Forge until the beginning of World War Two. Sport had already become a main interest in the life of the young lad and with a boxing boom in the valley it wasn't long before Stan came to the attention of the well-informed fight fraternity. As a tough, aggressive fighter, he had beaten everyone at flyweight and bantamweight to become a leading contender for the Welsh title. As with so many promising sportsmen at the time, war would intervene. A weight gain combined with a difficult life at sea would end his dreams of boxing immortality.

In 1942, at the age of twenty-one years, Stanley Bateman joined the Royal Navy and was awarded the Distinguished Service Medal for bravery on the shores of Sicily. His citation states:

> 'AB Bateman took part in a series of hazardous operations in the Mediterranean between March, 1943 and the end of 1945, when he was a seaman gunner on HMLCI 278. He helped in troop landing operations in North Africa, Sicily, Italy (including the Anzio beachhead) and Elba. The normal carrying capacity of the craft was 200, but at times they carried up to 700. The crew numbered sixteen. AB Bateman's craft was often first ashore in these landings - and Bateman himself was the first to land. It was his job to carry the line ashore so that the troops could land, and it was his gallantry in a series of these actions that won him the decoration.'

It was in 1942 Able Seaman Bateman, through a chance encounter in Naples, met his brother Eddie, who became a Squadron Leader in Coastal Command. This pleasant reunion would be supplemented by the surprise arrival of a number of young men who were also from the Pontnewynydd district.

Stan returned to his occupation in the Pontnewynydd Forge where he worked until it closed down. The remainder of his working life was spent at the Royal Ordnance Factory, Glascoed.

Although still in school, a pretty young local girl, one Margaret Isobel Lodge, had a part-time job of delivering milk and Stan's mother was one of her favourite customers. Often Mrs Bateman would mention her youngest son, or produce a letter received from him that very morning. 'Bella' was six years younger than Stan and good number of years passed before she set eyes on him at the end of the long war. A romance blossomed and they married on October 4, 1947 at St. Alban's Church, Pontypool. The issue of this happy union was a daughter Lorraine and one son, Richard.

This courageous man lived happily watching his young family growing up and enjoying the sporting scene while a committee member of the Pontnewynydd Forge Club. He passed away on December 15, 1984, at the age of 64 years.

# HAROLD SAMUEL BEACHAM
**Military Medal**

Bethel George Beacham, of 9 Cross Street, Blaenavon, a timberman in the local colliery, produced five boys and three girls. His son Harold S. Beacham was born August 2, 1916, and with his brothers and sisters he attended Hillside Infants School and later the Blaenavon Endowed School. His first employment after completing his education was in the newsagents of George Rees, Blaenavon, but an aptitude for carpentry would lead him to become a skilled French Polisher. When twenty-three years old, and employed in this trade, he was called up while living in Birmingham.

In March 1940, as part of the South Wales Borderers Regiment, he trained with his brother Frank at Brecon. After training, both brothers joined the Brecknock Battalion of the South Wales Borderers before Harold was transferred to the Regiment of the 1st Battalion, The Gordon Highlanders, in 1942. He served with distinction throughout the North Africa campaign. A dispatch from an officer told of the cool courage of the young Blaenavon man and explained how he led a trapped platoon to safety through a dense minefield during the Eighth Army's advance against Rommel's forces. The dispatch states:

> *'For reconnoitring a route out of a dense minefield through a thick pall of smoke and with shrapnel flying all about him, so that he could lead the remainder of his trapped platoon to safety, Lance Corporal Beacham, of the Gordon Highlanders, was awarded the Military Medal.*
>
> *During the attack on the Buerat position on the way to Tripoli, Lance Corporal Beacham's platoon suddenly found itself in the midst of a dense anti-tank and anti-personnel minefield. The mines were exploding in all directions, and two of the first casualties were the Platoon Commander and Sergeant. The enemy were also laying a heavy mortar fire on the trapped men.*
>
> *Lance Corporal Beacham instantly realised that the safety of the platoon lay in his hands. He therefore reconnoitered, found a safe route, returned to the remnants of his company and led them out of the minefield without losing a single man on the way.'*

Later in the war he received shrapnel wounds in both kidneys and after demobilisation one was removed.

After the war Harold worked for the Blaenavon Company laying railway tracks. He married Eileen Whitcombe, of Forge Side, and they had three sons, Robert, Paul and Graham. He continued to enjoy carpentry projects during his leisure time, but sadly, due to his wartime injury, he died on August 3, 1965, at the young age of forty-nine years. This man of magnificent courage is buried at Varteg Road Cemetery.

# JOHN WILLIAM BEVAN
## Military Medal

John William Bevan senior, a collier hardened by the immensely physical work underground, lived most of his married life at 36, Ty Pwcca Estate, Cwmbran. Four sons and two daughters would be the issue of a happy marriage. One of his sons would bring honour to the district towards the end of World War Two.

Born August 31, 1917, and named John William Bevan, after his father, this fit young man first joined his father in colliery work before his love of horses took him to France where he served as an apprentice in a racing stable. With this experience, he returned home and was fortunate to find work on the surface of Blaendare Colliery as an ostler.

Following the outbreak of war John Bevan joined the Army on January 17, 1940, and served six years as a Gunner in the Royal Artillery. On February 21, 1942, he arrived home from the dangers of war to marry Ann Poole, a young lady from Upper Cwmbran. The marriage, like so many others at that difficult time, took place in Pontypool Registry Office, and two sons, Alan John and Aden Terence, were born later.

While in Italy 965218 Gunner Bevan faced danger on a number of occasions, but none so intense as in November 1944. An officer of the 4th Polish Army Regiment reported the action for which he immediately received the Military Medal:

> 'On the 5th November 1944 one of the tanks of the 4th Polish Armed Regiment was knocked out by an enemy bazooka at Marsignano, one of the crew being killed and two wounded.
> Gunner Bevan who was a maintenance signaller with an O.P. party supporting a squadron of the Regiment, immediately went to the assistance of the crew although the road leading to the tank was under heavy mortar and MG fire and the tank itself was only about 20 yards from the enemy position. Regardless of his own danger he remained by the side of the tank

*giving first aid to the crew, although he was still under fire, and then returned to report the circumstances to the Polish Squadron Commander.'*

Due to the difficult times his gallantry medal, reported in the *London Gazette* on April 26, 1945, was forwarded to him with a form of receipt to be signed and returned to the War Office. Meanwhile, at a meeting of the Urban District Council of Cwmbran, it was resolved to send a letter of congratulation to number 2, The Garw, Croesyceiliog, the home of Gunner Bevan. Prior to this Mrs Bevan knew nothing of her husband's brave action until reporters from several newspapers knocked on her door.

After six years and one hundred and thirty seven days of service with the colours in North Africa and Italy, and his conduct described as exemplary, John W. Bevan took his discharge and returned home. For a further three years he served in the army reserve.

A keen sportsman, as a young man he played a good game of rugby for Croesyceiliog RFC, and became a life-long supporter while serving for many years on the club's committee. After thirty-six years employment at the nearby Panteg Steelworks, he became the proud recipient of a long service certificate. This brave and caring man died December 4th, 1988, age 71 years, and was buried in the grounds of the ancient Siloam Baptist Chapel, Upper Cwmbran.

# ALBERT JOHN BOOTH
**Military Cross**

Born 1919, at Tredegar Street, Risca, Albert John Booth would become a popular hero. His father, in search of work, brought his family to Cwmbran in 1934. While living at Yew Tree Inn, Fred Charles Booth became an employee of Saunders Valve Ltd, Cwmbran, and remained in this secure employment for the rest of his working life.

Albert John Booth left school to take up employment at Spittle's Foundry, Newport, and he remained at the works until joining the Welsh Guards in 1938. As a sergeant in this famous regiment he was very prominent in the rear guard action at Dunkirk.

On June 2, 1941, the guardsman married Rouine, an attractive young French lady, at Llantarnam Church, Cwmbran. They would have a son, Darrel.

Sergeant Booth's military career changed on the day a fellow soldier suggested that he should accompany him on an officer-training course. The young Cwmbran man easily passed his examinations to become Lieutenant Booth of the South Wales Borderers. Unfortunately, his friend found the course too difficult and failed to qualify.

In September 1944, the conspicuous gallantry of Lieutenant A.J. Booth led to the immediate award of the Military Cross. On December 29, 1944 the *London Gazette* officially announced the award and his citation reads:

> *'On 10th September 1944, during the assault on the outer defences of Le Havre, Lieutenant Booth was commanding the leading platoon of 'B' Company.*
> *This platoon ran into the defensive fire of the enemy, where it was compelled to remain owing to the position of the forward Company. Lieutenant Booth during that time remained for the most part, standing upright, walking from section to section, and by his magnificent example*

*maintained a remarkable steadiness in his platoon. Throughout the whole of this time Lieutenant Booth kept his Company Commander fully informed of the state of things in front.*

*Later that night Lieutenant Booth attacked the final objective, supported by flame-throwers. His skill and bravery resulted in the capture of the position and of forty prisoners, without loss to his platoon. His example was an inspiration to all ranks under his command.'*

Although wounded in the leg, the young officer soon returned to active service. A letter from King George VI informed that he could not personally present the award and the coveted medal was sent to Lieutenant Booth's wife.

After the war A.J. Booth became employed as a foreman at the iron works of Guest, Keen and Nettlefolds, Cwmbran. Following his retirement the old soldier would be seen carrying out a leisurely part-time job at the Cwmbran Boating Lake. He had won many medals in the army for boxing and he kept his interest in the sport throughout his life. Always a keen member of the Cwmbran British Legion, he was to be known further afield as the active secretary of Cwmbran Darts League.

This well thought of soldier who made the difficult and commendable rise through the ranks to become a commissioned officer, died in May 1997, at the age of 78 years.

# DENNIS RONALD BOWERS
## Conspicuous Gallantry Medal (Flying)

In March 1945, the heavily laden bomber took off with its pilot, Flying Officer Hampson, at the controls. He had been ordered to attack Harpenerweg. Among the crew was thirty-year-old Dennis Bowers, the only son of Mr. G. Bowers, the Highway, New Inn, Pontypool.

Before the war Dennis Bowers grew up in the Panteg district while attending St. Alban's School and Newport High School. Employed as an optician in Newport, it was a blissful life for the young man, but war intervened and like so many men he felt it his duty to volunteer in May 1940. Three months later he was called up and began his training in the Royal Air Force. By 1942, he had fallen in love with a young lady who lived locally. He married Miss Betty Bevan, of Woodside Road, Cwmbran, the same year, and began a long and happy marriage.

Already accustomed to great danger, Flight Sergeant Bowers boarded the bomber with the rest of the crew. As flight engineer he did an instrument check as the large aeroplane roared into life. It would be his last flight.

When approaching the designated target it was observed that the anti-aircraft fire was particularly fierce and all on board knew they were in for a difficult time. With the target getting near, there was suddenly a loud explosion and they had been hit by heavy flak. Sergeant Bowers was severely wounded in the leg, but in spite of this he remained at his post.

In no time at all another shell burst underneath the aircraft and caused extensive damage. Sergeant Bowers sustained further injury; his leg almost severed. A large opening had this time appeared in the bottom of the aircraft and the injured man was in immediate danger of falling out. Crewmembers quickly caught hold of him as he balanced precariously on the jagged metal. Pulled to safety, and grievously wounded, he remained fully determined to be of assistance. It took every ounce of strength to get near his instrument panel. When in position he kept his pilot advised of the remaining fuel, and gave directions regarding the changing of respective fuel tanks. This support was of tremendous help to the pilot, who was struggling to keep control of the badly damaged aircraft. Finally, the plane succeeded in reaching Britain and an airfield was found before an emergency landing took place.

Flight Sergeant Bowers, although grievously injured, set a magnificent example of courage, fortitude, and devotion to duty and his example would be long remembered by the other members of his squadron.

While in a South Wales RAF hospital recovering from serious wounds and a leg amputation, the young man from New Inn received news of the award of the Conspicuous Gallantry Medal. His pilot received the DFC and two other members of the crew, the DFM for their conduct on that particular flight.

Dennis Bowers attended a popular emergency teaching course after the war and taught for many years at Wern School, Sebastopol, Torfaen. He retired as a head of department at the school and many of his pupils still remember with great affection this quiet, brave, caring man.

# HUGH W. BRACE
### Mentioned in Dispatches

Born 1920, at Talywain, near Pontypool, Monmouthshire. The son of Amy Elizabeth and William Brace, a respected carpenter and funeral director, young Hugh attended Garndiffaith School before entering Abersychan Secondary School. Prior to joining the British Army he was a student at Birmingham University.

For four long years Hugh Brace served with the Royal Artillery in the Middle East and Central Mediterranean. It was in September 1945 when Sergeant Brace received confirmation that he had deservedly been Mentioned in Dispatches for outstanding services from May 1 to August 31, 1944. The account of his good work reads:

> 'At this time his Regiment was supporting the Royal Fusiliers at the crossing of the Rapido River in Italy. Sergeant Brace was sent forward with a party to clear enemy machine gun posts. They accomplished their task, and though depleted in strength, went forward with the infantry in the attack.'

With the war ended he returned safely home and in the Autumn of 1948, married Ceridwin Cecil, in the district of Abergavenny. Two children, a boy and girl, were the issue of the long and happy marriage. Hugh immediately commenced employment with the Patent Office, Chancery Lane, London. He remained in the same interesting occupation all his working life and retired in 1980 at the age of sixty years. In his younger days the former Talywain man was a keen tennis and squash player and very much enjoyed foreign travel with his family. At the age of 84 years Hugh Brace lives at Farnborough, Kent, and is still very much full of life with a lively sense of humour.

# GEORGE RICHARD BRADLEY
### Distinguished Flying Medal

One of the three sons born to Mr and Mrs George Bradley, of Wern Road, Sebastopol, near Pontypool, George R. Bradley became a modest hero in the dark and frightening times of World War Two. George junior attended Wern Council School before completing his education at the West Monmouthshire School, Pontypool. While at the senior school he became interested in the Royal Air Force, mainly through the Air Training Corp, which was open to all interested pupils. The keen sixteen-year old completed his education in 1936 and immediately commenced an apprenticeship at R.A.F. Halton. Standing over six feet tall, he soon won several medals for boxing and played rugby for his Station. George  completed the exacting three-year training course just prior to the outbreak of war. An immediate posting abroad, followed by the gradual rise in rank to Flight Sergeant, preceded the presentation of the Distinguished Flying Medal by King George VI in May 1943. By this time Flight Sergeant Bradley had taken part in forty-eight operational flights over Germany (including the 1,000-bomber raid on Cologne), Italy and occupied territory. The official citation reads:

> 'Throughout a large number of successful operational sorties against important and heavily defended targets, Flight Sergeant Bradley has shown courage and coolness of a very high degree. His skill and efficiency have enabled him to complete his allotted tasks and his keenness have been a fine example to the squadron.'

While on leave in July 1943, the people of the village of Sebastopol presented their hero with an inscribed gold watch in appreciation of his tremendous courage.

George Bradley received his commission six weeks before attending the Investiture ceremony at Buckingham Palace. The welcome promotion to Pilot Officer was coupled with the posting to ground duties, an arrangement the young man found very disagreeable. Following repeated requests, Pilot Officer George R. Bradley, DFM, received his greatest wish and returned to operational flights. Sadly, the brave young pilot, who had played his full part in the defence of our country, was soon to be reported missing in action on the 29th August 1944. He is buried with six other airmen of the Royal Air Force in the Norre Vorupor Cemetery, Denmark.

# WILLIAM KENNETH BRANCH
### Distinguished Flying Cross

Born at Abersychan in 1912, the son of Mr. Hedley Branch, managing director of an Abersychan firm of builders. Early education took place at a Pontypool school and later in Clarence School, Weston-super-Mare and Denstone College, Staffordshire. After completing his education the young man went to Canada for four years where he was employed in the inspection department of the Northern Electric Company. He returned to this country to join the Royal Air Force in 1933. Three years later he again went abroad, serving in a bomber squadron in Iraq and Palestine, where he was when the 2nd World War commenced.

Mostly as a navigator with 107 Squadron, the Abersychan man took part in an amazing eighty-nine dangerous operational flights and he was determined to complete one hundred flights. Alas, it was not to be. Grievously wounded by flak in the left forearm immediately after dropping bombs on a target at Rennes, France, and in great pain and continuously loosing blood, the courageous valley man thought his last hour had come. Fighting against sinking into unconsciousness he continued to navigate his plane. After an agonising eighty minutes the aircraft landed safely at an airfield in this country. In August 1943, Flying Officer Branch was awarded the Distinguished Flying Cross for his outstanding courage and determination. The citation reads:

> 'In August, 1943, F/O Branch was the navigator of the leading aircraft of a formation detailed to attack a target at Rennes. He successfully guided the pilot to the objective over difficult country, and bombed the target in face of fierce opposition. Immediately after the bombs were released the aircraft was hit and damaged, and F/O Branch was wounded. In spite of very great pain and loss of blood he navigated his aircraft back to an airfield in this country, and on arrival displayed the greatest fortitude while being extricated from the aircraft. Throughout the whole operation F/O Branch displayed outstanding courage and determination.'

Previously married in March 1943, to Edna Trow, a young lady from Middlesborough, F/O Branch would have many visits while in hospital.

Unfortunately, he never regained complete use of the fingers of his left hand. In May 1945, Flying Officer William Kenneth Branch attended Buckingham Palace where King George VI invested him with the Distinguished Flying Cross.

After the war this very brave and highly respected young man moved his family to the City of Cardiff where he worked and watched his young family growing up.

# THEODORE ALBERT CASELEY
### Distinguished Flying Medal

Born August 1917, in Cwmbran village, T.A. Caseley was the eldest of three brothers and two sisters. His father Albert worked for a time as a collier at Hafodrynys Colliery and later in the Girlings Factory, Cwmbran. Early education took place at St. Dial's School and later a period of four years was spent at the West Monmouthshire School, Pontypool. Work as a collier at Crumlin Valley Colliery became the young man's occupation for four years after leaving school, and his leisure time was spent mostly as a member of the Cwmbran Territorial Army band.

As a territorial with the 2nd Monmouthshire Regiment he was mobilised at the outbreak of war, but after serving for one month it became necessary for him to return to the colliery. Later he volunteered for aircrew duties with the Royal Air Force.

Over thirty extremely dangerous operational flights as a navigator earned the Cwmbran man the Distinguished Flying Medal. The official citation reads:

> 'Sergeant Caseley, throughout his tour of operational duty has displayed praiseworthy efficiency as a navigator. In raids on most of the heavily fortified objectives in Germany and during mine-laying sorties, his endeavours have contributed largely to the success achieved by his crew. His keenness, enthusiasm and skill have earned the respect of his fellow navigators.'

Accompanied by his mother and father, he was presented with the award by King George VI at Buckingham Palace in September 1943. At home he received a letter of congratulations from the Cwmbran Urban District Council. This was soon followed by a supper prepared by the ladies committee of the Cwmbran Urban District Band, in celebration of his high award. Prior to the war Albert had been an accomplished euphonium player with this popular band. With his mother as a guest of honour, he gratefully received a wallet, inscribed with his initials, from Chairman of the Committee, Councillor W.G. Thomas.

T.A. Caseley returned to duty and after a further period of training he became a Pilot Officer. Sadly, the war took it toll on the Caseley family. The hero's third brother Sapper Roy Caseley was killed in a road accident in 1940, shortly after returning from Dunkirk. Another brother, Pilot Officer R. Job Caseley, a member of the Pathfinder Squadron was lost over Leipzig, Germany.

Theodore Albert Caseley married Joan Curley, a local girl at Llantarnam Church, Cwmbran. They would have a son Howell and two girls, Jeanette and Gina. After the war Albert worked as a pilot for a civil airline and flew the British Prime Minister to America in the nineteen-fifties. Later he developed an ear condition, which forced him to give up flying and work in Air Control at Heathrow Airport. He completed his working life with Custom and Exercise at Newport Docks, Gwent.

Albert died in December 1977 and is buried at Panteg Cemetery, Torfaen.

# LLEWELLYN REDVERS CATER
**Mentioned in Dispatches**

Born July 4th, 1902, in the Pontypool district, the second son of Ada and William Thomas Cater, of 29, Percy Street, Garndiffaith, Monmouthshire. Llewellyn Cater attended the Garndiffaith Council School before working for while at Varteg Colliery. In April 1921, he joined the British Army and had a long and distinguished career. During leave from the Army, he married Miss Blodwen Owen, a local girl, at Pisgah Chapel, Garndiffaith, on October 1, 1927. The long and happy union produced three sons, Douglas, Philip and Brian.

As a member of the Royal Regiment of Artillery he went to India in December 1932, and was accompanied by his wife and two children. His youngest son, Brian, was born in India, and, incidentally, became the first European child to be christened at Agra Baptist Church. They returned to Garndiffaith on leave in 1938 after over five years abroad with the 7th Medium Regiment.

The young Garndiffaith man made a commendable rise through the ranks and soon after the commencement of World War Two, he narrowly escaped capture in the retreat from Dunkirk. After a short rest, Captain Cater was ordered to the Middle East, and served in Cyprus, Palestine, Iraq, Syria and Libya. After Rommel's push to the outskirts of Alexandria he was admitted to hospital, and on discharge re-applied for posting to his old Regiment. This was granted and with his Regiment he went to Europe on D-Day. It was during the North Africa campaign that Captain (Quarter Master) L.R. Cater, Royal Artillery, was deservedly Mentioned in Dispatches for gallant and distinguished services.

When the war ended he had the tremendous responsibility of distributing food to the starving German people. After thirty-five years serving his country Major Cater retired from the Army and eventually returned to his roots. For a while he was part of a team carrying out confidential work at Porton Down before working for short periods at the British Nylon Spinners, Pontypool, and the Royal

Ordnance Factory, Glascoed. At this time he lived at Maesderwin, Pontypool and later at Llanyrafon, Cwmbran.

In his younger days he played rugby in the Army and excelled at hockey. Always a strong family man he and his wife celebrated their golden wedding at the Somerton Hotel, Cwmbran in 1977.

This brave man who had given so much to the defence of his country over a long period of time passed away on July 29, 1978.

# MURRELL CHATWIN
## Military Medal

The son of Mr and Mrs J. Chatwin, of 55, Richmond Road, Pontnewydd, Cwmbran, Murrell Chatwin became a railway employee with his three brothers and father. Before the war Newport RFC had groomed him for a Welsh cap, but the war and circumstances curtailed his rugby career. Often, the fit young man would cycle to Aberbeeg to act as a relief railway porter until 12 mid-day on Saturdays, and then play in a top class rugby match in the afternoon. It was a happy time in the young man's life, which was further enhanced by his marriage in 1939 to Miss Ruby Pearson, of Upper Cwmbran.

Murrell has never forgotten the day when his call-up papers dropped through the letterbox. It was June 13th, 1940, and he would go through almost five years of bitter fighting. In Italy, during June 1945, Sergeant Chatwin brought honour to the Welsh Guards with his bravery and determination. This was later recorded in the official history of the regiment:

> 'The Country is flat, closely cultivated and for the most part hedgeless, but it is intersected by irrigation ditches and thin rows of slender poplars which mark the boundaries of farms or line the lanes connecting them. For operational purposes key points had been christened with the names of a bevy of ladies – Mary, Charlotte, Alice, Juliet, etc. – to be captured by the Guardsmen, and were chalked on their maps. Among the first away was Sergeant M. G. Chatwin, commanding a platoon of No. 4 Company, and by a combination of skilful leadership and unskilful map reading he managed to be at least one lady ahead of his named objective. Leading his platoon with great skill and bravery, he directed them in attacks on six in turn and covered a distance of over five miles.'

For his good work he was awarded the Military Medal. Murrel Chatwin returned home and continues to live in Pontnewydd, Cwmbran. He has a daughter Linda who regularly visits her father. Many years later Murrell went on holiday to Italy and passed the river Po, the area where he had thoroughly earned his award. It would be a time of many quiet memories.

# GERALD COLLINS
## Distinguished Service Medal

Born June 15, 1915, in the district of Pontypool. His father was a foreman with the local Council and he had an older brother Daniel and sister Bridget. He lost both his parents before the age of fourteen years of age. Educated at Garndiffaith Council School and Abersychan Technical School, a post of apprentice fitter with a local omnibus company soon became available. He progressed well under the patronage of Mr. W.J. Barret, of Barret's Omnibus Company, who gave every encouragement to the orphan.

At the age of eighteen years he joined the Royal Navy as a stoker and promotion came quickly to the young Garndiffaith lad. After nine months he became a first class stoker and in just three years he had passed the examination qualifying him for the rank of engine room artificer, a petty officer rating. This promotion probable made him one of the youngest petty officers in the Royal Navy and the fact did not go unnoticed in Garndiffaith. While home on leave from H.M.S. Nelson the popular young seaman was given a smoking concert at the White Hart Inn, Abersychan, where he was presented with a gold wristlet watch from the staff of Barrett's Omnibus Company and a silver pencil from the proprietor.

Petty Officer Gerald Collins went on to receive several commendations during his career and just before his twenty seventh birthday, in June 1942, he was awarded the coveted Distinguished Service Medal while serving in His Majesties submarines. He received the award from King George VI at Buckingham Palace in July 1942. He later served on a variety of ships and became a Chief Engine Room Artificer before discharging from the Royal Navy.

After the war the married, former seaman, worked at British Nylon Spinners, Pontypool, as a construction fitter and became a supervisor. He transferred to I.C.I. Gloucester in 1963 and retired in 1974. He spoke very little about his wartime experiences and spent his leisure time enjoying sport, travelling and reading.

At the age of 73 years this reticent man passed away at his home, 14, Penny Orchard, Upton St. Leonard's, Gloucester. Not long after his wife Maisie returned to her hometown of Blaenavon.

# ALFRED GEORGE COOPER
## Mentioned in Military Orders

Born 1908 at Sebastopol, near Pontypool, Monmouthshire. The son of William and Emily Cooper, 7, Austin Road, Sebastopol, he attended the nearby Panteg Wern Council School. Like most boys born alongside the large Panteg Ironworks, it was easy to find employment. Soon he would be working alongside his father in the backbreaking industry. In his spare time the fit young man became a member of the Territorial Army attached to the Panteg Battery, and showed a special aptitude for military work. For seventeen years he served as a part-time soldier during which time he and his wife Francis had two children, David and Margaret.

In 1939, Alf Cooper went to war. By 1942, the 34-year-old Sebastopol man had served in Britain and Northern Ireland before going overseas. On a sunny day in August 1942, the Sebastopol man showed great coolness and courage, which earned him a Mention in Military Orders. The citation, made by the Army Commander, South Eastern Army, reads:

> 'On an occasion in August 1942, when bombs were dropped by the enemy at a South-East coast town, causing damage and casualties, 770310 B.J.M.S. A. Cooper, of the Field Regiment, R.A., displayed commendable coolness and courage. With complete disregard of danger from collapsing walls he crawled in among the debris and gave very material help in the rescue of those trapped in the fallen buildings.'

It would be quite a while before his wife, living at 'Arosfa,' Greenhill Road, Sebastopol, became aware of her husbands bravery.

At the end of the war B.Q.M.S. Cooper returned home and resumed his employment in the nearby ironworks. At times he would complete small building projects for local people for a reasonable cost and remained well liked and respected throughout his life.

# SAMUEL EDGAR COWEN
## Distinguished Flying Medal

Born 1920 at Pontypool, the youngest son of Mr
and Mrs S. J. Cowen, of 11 Edward Street,
Pontypool. Sam and his brother and two sisters
attended the local junior school before he
completed his education at the nearby West
Monmouthshire School. After leaving school
in August 1935, he immediately joined the
Royal Air Force and took up an apprentiship.

By 1942, the young Pontypool man had
become a Flight Sergeant with No. 149
Squadron and was participating in many
dangerous flights into enemy territory. One
particularly difficult flight resulted in the
Distinguished Flying Medal being awarded to
568233 Flight Sergeant Cowen. The
announcement was made in the November 3,
1942, issue of the *London* Gazette and his full citation states:

> '*Sergeant Cowen has completed 29 successful operational sorties. His work
> throughout his operational tour has been very commendable and worthy of
> recognition.*
>
> *On one particular occasion when returning from Mainz on 12th
> September, 1942, his machine was badly damaged by a fighter attack.
> Working with great coolness he successfully extinguished two small fires, one
> in the fuselage and one in the Port Inner Engine. The weather on return
> was hazardous, the machine becoming badly iced up, but Sergeant Cowen
> worked on coolly.*
>
> *Through his hard work and efficiency he aided the crew to bring the
> aircraft back to this country, finally winding the undercarriage down by
> hand. The machine, despite his efforts, had to be crash landed through
> petrol shortage.*'

In 1943, and accompanied by his sister, Flight Sergeant Samuel Edgar Cowen
attended an investiture in Buckingham Palace and received the Distinguished
Flying Medal from King George VI.

Between his dangerous missions Sam met and fell in love with Leading
Aircraft Woman Kay Macaulay, WAAF. They married in 1944 at St. Andrew's

Church, Earlsfield, London. Best man, Flying Officer R.D. Morrison, remembers well the happy event and the splendid dinner party given by the newly-weds in the evening at the Cumberland Hotel, Marble Arch, London. Two sons, Keith and Gareth, was the result of the happy union.

Sam Cohen decided on a career in the Royal Air Force and became a Squadron Leader, while his wife enjoyed her work with the South East Gas Board. Much of his leisure time was taken up serving the London Welsh Rugby Club in various posts. Sadly, he died at a young age in RAF Hospital, Uxbridge, Middlesex, on February 2, 1972.

# LESLIE WYNDHAM CRUM
### Distinguished Flying Cross

The son of Mr. W.A. Crum, a local steelworks foreman, Leslie Wyndham Crum was born on the 27 August 1920, in the ancient parish of Panteg. He and his two brothers and four sisters attended Griffithstown Council School. Wyndham did well in the junior school and moved on to spend time at Abersychan Technical School. This was followed by a prestigious move to the Merchant Ventura's College, Bristol, which greatly influenced his future career. The young man was in the right place to commence his first employment as a student in the Bristol Aeroplane Company (Engine Division).

Prior to enlisting he was employed in the Research Department of a Government Factory. In 1941, and at the age of twenty-one years, the Griffithstown man joined the Royal Air Force and served his country well until 1946. Between 1941 and 1942, he attended observer training and received a commission after achieving first place at No. 2 Air Observers School, Edmonton, Canada. Trainees who received their observer's wing were ready to take their place with operational squadrons of the Royal Air Force. What followed for Wyndham were two tours in Bomber Command on 100, 625 and 170 Squadrons.

In September 1943, Wyndham married a delightful young lady who went by the name of Madge Goodall. The wedding took place at Keighley, Yorkshire, and the issue of this happy union would be a daughter, Judith Anne, and a son Wyndham Robin.

Returning to duty, several months passed before Flying Officer Crum was heartened to read the following extract in the London Gazette dated 7 December 1943:

'The King has been graciously pleased to approve the following award in recognition of gallantry and devotion to duty in the execution of air operations:

### Distinguished Flying Cross

### Flying Officer Leslie Wyndham Crum (129358)
### Royal Air Force Volunteer Reserve, No. 100 Squadron

*This officer has taken part as navigator in a number of important operations. Setting his mind fearlessly on the task in hand, he displayed a fine fighting spirit. On a sortie to Hamburg in July, 1943, the aircraft was badly damaged by an enemy night fighter. Two of the crew were killed and one wounded but the navigational skill displayed by Flying Officer Crum enabled his pilot to fly safely to base. By his ability to make the correct decision in emergency and his cool judgement in the face of heavy odds, this officer has proved of great value to his crew.'*

During November 1945, King George VI and Queen Elizabeth paid a visit of two days to Wales during which His Royal Highness decorated Flying Officer Crum, of 6 Asquith Street, Griffithstown, with the Distinguished Flying Cross. The Investiture was held at the City Hall, Cardiff.

In the years that followed war, Wyndham became senior manager and consultant in engine design for Rolls Royce, Derby. Leisure time spent with his family, coupled with an interest in rugby, birdwatching and travel, filled many happy hours for this modest local hero.

# RONALD CUMBLEY
## Mentioned in Dispatches

Ron Cumbley had always been known to lead a life of compassion and this was witnessed on a fateful day in September 1941. His parents, William Henry and Florence Cumbley, of Pontnewydd, had conducted a business of decorators in Pontypool, Griffithstown and Pontnewydd, while Ron grew up in the Eastern Valley before joining the Royal Engineers. He had met and married a young lady from Newton Abbot, Devon, but the war had spoiled their peaceful existence.

Corporal Cumbley, age 35 years, observed two children who had strayed into a coast minefield and immediately went to help. Fully aware of the danger, his thoughts were for the safety of the children, and although extra careful of his approach, a mine did its job, but unfortunately not against the enemy. The caring man died immediately and was buried at Kingsteignton (St. Michael) Churchyard, Devon.

It would be the following year when the late Corporal's widow, Mrs Hilda Mary Cumbley, of Dawlish, received a certificate of her husband's bravery, which is inscribed:

> 'By the King's Order, the name of Corporal R. Cumbley, Royal Engineers, was published in the "London Gazette," and commended for brave conduct. I am charged to record his Majesty's appreciation of the services rendered.
>
> Signed: David Margesson.'

# LEONARD JOHN CUNNINGHAM
## Military Medal – Croix de Guerre – Mentioned in Dispatches

Born January 19, 1919, at Cwmbran. His father Thomas Cunningham raised his young family at 16, Spring Street, Forgehammer, while working in the nearby iron works of Guest, Keen and Nettlefolds. Leonard, with his four brothers and four sisters, attended the Roman Catholic School, Cwmbran, before he joined his father at work in the iron works. His father had been a Sergeant Major in the Great War and this in all probability led to the Cunningham boys becoming part-time soldiers with the 2nd Monmouthshire Regiment before the outbreak of war in 1939.

4077099 Sergeant Leonard John Cunningham served six years and 253 days with the colours and during this time he received a Certificate of Merit and was twice decorated for gallantry.

His Certificate of Merit was given for service in operations near the Albert Canal, Belgium. Later, in May 1945, he was awarded the Croix de Guerre for 'services rendered in the liberation of France.' This would be followed in April by yet another award for bravery when the Cwmbran man received the Military Medal for bravery in North-West Europe. The citation states:

> 'On the 16th April, 1945, during the attack on Kukenmoor, Germany, Sgt. Cunningham was commanding one of the leading platoons. In spite of extremely heavy and accurate small arms fire, which caused a number of casualties, Sgt. Cunningham led his platoon across 300 yards of open ground to his objective. It was undoubtedly due to his great courage and leadership that the objective was reached.
>
> Having reorganised his platoon Sgt. Cunningham observed that the platoon on his left was pinned down short of the Company objective and was suffering heavy casualties which included the Platoon Commander and all the NCOs. He directed the fire of his own platoon at the enemy holding up the platoon on his left and handing over his command to the next senior,

*went over to it. He took command and, under very heavy fire reorganised and led it to its objective.*

*Sgt. Cunningham's great personal courage and initiative were directly responsible for securing the Company's objective and had a considerable influence on the Battalion successfully taking their objective.'*

Sergeant Cunningham was sent his medal with a personal letter from King George VI.

While on leave in 1945, the Cwmbran hero married Beryl Francis Cordier in the Roman Catholic Church. They would have three children Lyn, Steve and Diane.

After the war Len returned to his former employment at the local ironworks. He continued his service as a part-time soldier until the late nineteen sixties. A man of moderation he enjoyed a pint of beer in the Rifleman's Club, Cwmbran, and followed all kinds of sport. It was a particular pleasure for him and his wife to attend the regularly held Territorial Army dances. This man of great courage died on June 14, 1975, at the young age of 55 years.

# LEON DAVIES
## Military Medal

Leon (Leo) Davies, of Talywain, attended the local school and worked at Blaensychan Colliery before joining the British Army in 1932. He would see action on the northwest frontier of India, Iraq and the Middle East. At Tobruk he was captured and placed in an Italian prisoner-of-war camp. The Italians were good to him, but he had already made up his mind to escape some time before they capitulated. Guarded by the Germans he made his escape, was recaptured and made three more daring escapes before losing his pursuers.

For courage, the name No. 3908403 Private (Acting Corporal) Leon Davies, South Wales Borderers, appeared in the June 13, 1944, edition of the *London Gazette* with the announcement that he had been awarded the Military Medal.

On his return home the people of Talywain honoured the young man with a special celebratory evening. Later, in September 1944, Acting Corporal Leon Davies received the Military Medal in Scotland at an Investiture by HM King George VI. His mother, Mrs G Williams, of 35, Fairfield, Talywain, heard her son described as "the man who defied the Germans four times." To this the King commented, "I admire your pluck."

Leon survived the war and led a long and productive life.

# RONALD DUDLEY DAVIES
### Mentioned in Dispatches

Born 1915, the son of Mr Ernest R. Davies and Councillor Margaret Davies, of Mill House, Pontnewynydd, Monmouthshire. Ron attended Cwmffrwdoer School and West Monmouthshire School until the age of fifteen years. As a youth everything appeared paltry and insignificant until the day, out of curiosity, he casually walked into Merchants Hill Baptist Church, Pontnewynydd. His aim was to join the popular youth club previously formed as an offshoot of the old Christian Endeavour Society. Soon, he pledged his life to Christian service and went on to the Theological College, Swansea. With the spirit of adventure very present in the young man's personality, in 1934, he went to Little Tibet as a missionary and obtained a great deal of experience among the native races.

*(Courtesy of Pontypool Museum)*

In 1942, as a cleric, he joined the Royal Army Service Corps attached to the Indian Army and quickly gained promotion to Captain. Further promotion to Major by 1945, coincided with the part he played in the push, which resulted in the capture of Rangoon. Early in September 1945, not only were his parents gladdened to hear he was safe and well, but that he had been Mentioned in Dispatches and decorated for gallant and distinguished service in the Burma campaign.

After the war Major Davies chose to support the World Wide Evangelists Crusade at a mission station in Kashmir. In 1947, a great deal of fighting and unrest in the area put the lives of many Europeans in great danger. Sadly, the thirty-three year old Pontnewynydd missionary was shot after saving the lives of three British women. While attempting to escape on horseback across a bridge, which crosses the River Jheium, fanatical Moslem Pathans killed him.

He was buried in a solitary grave within sight of the Mission House at Buniyar, Kashmir. In January 1948, there was a huge attendance at a service, not of mourning, but of thanksgiving for the martyred missionary in the Merchant Hill Baptist Church, Pontnewynydd, Monmouthshire. A memorial in the splendid church states:

*To the Glory of God in memory of*
*Ronald Dudley Davies*
*The first foreign missionary from this church who*
*gave his life for fellow missionaries in Kashmir, India,*
*on November 7th 1947, aged 33 years.*

Another less known memorial to this good man is a book on Ronald Davies' missionary work 'Lal Sahib', which was deposited in the library of his old school.

# WILFRED DEACON
## Mentioned in Dispatches

Wilfred Deacon, the eldest son of Mr and Mrs W. Deacon grew up in the Garndiffaith district and attended the West Monmouthshire School, Pontypool. He later entered the Monmouthshire Training College, Caerleon. Before World War Two he was on the staff of Caerleon Boys' Endowed School and took an active part in the social life of Caerleon. As an enthusiastic member of the local amateur dramatic society he became its hard working secretary. He was also a member of the Caerleon tennis and cricket clubs. He met and married the daughter of Mr and Mrs W.H. Dean, Caerleon, and they had a son Jonathan.

In 1941, Mrs Deacon received a certificate signed by Captain the Rt. Hon. H.D.R. Margesson, MC., Secretary of State for War, recording the fact that in the July 26, 1940, supplement to the *London Gazette*, the name of Lieutenant (Acting Captain) Wilfred Deacon, an officer of the Royal Monmouthshire Royal Engineers was mentioned *'in recognition of distinguished services rendered in connection with operations in the field up to March 1940.'*

The regiment's history records:

> *'The march out of Cassel was attempted by night – a lovely night, made beautiful by the song of the nightingales which had not been driven from their haunts by the noise of the battle…With the first light, planes spotted the move and mortar fire directed at the column soon caused disorder, and troops took cover. Near Watou, Captain W. Deacon, and interpreter Jean Streichemberges received wounds, which incapacitated them. Captain W. Deacon was picked up by a German Field Ambulance before going to Oflag VII C at Laufen on the River Inn.'*

After the war Wilfred Deacon returned to his post of headmaster of Llanvaches School, near Penhow, but later took up a position with the British Broadcasting Company, London. He is known to have worked in the library of the BBC for many years.

# JOHN EDWARDS
## Military Medal

John Edwards, the son of Ellen and George Edwards, of Wesley Street, Cwmbran, grew up in the small village while attending St. Mary's Roman Catholic School. At eighteen years of age he became determined to join up and embarked on a career as a professional soldier.

Sergeant John Edwards had been in the Regular Army for fourteen years prior to 1945. For nine of these years he was stationed in India and Burma. His service abroad had been interrupted with a period of time based in England, where he met a young lady in Yeovil and married her in the picturesque town.

For 'courage, coolness and determination in action,' in March 1945, he was awarded the Military Medal by General Sir Oliver Leese, KCB, DSO, Commander-in-Chief Allied Land Forces, South-East Asia. The citation states:

> 'In Burma, Sergeant Edwards was No. 1 of a gun engaging the enemy. After the first ranging, the gun position was subjected to heavy enemy firing, the first shell falling two yards away from Sergeant Edwards's gun pit. Fragments struck and damaged the piece. Without hesitation, Sergeant Edwards continued to fire. The example set by his coolness and leadership was an inspiration to his detachment. Although it became necessary to replenish ammunition from outside the gun-pit, Sergeant Edwards so organised and controlled his detachment, composed largely of men in action for the first time, that this was done without a casualty. Throughout the whole period, the example shown by Sergeant Edwards, his courage and determination, was of the highest order.'

Mrs Ethel Rose Edwards received a copy of her husband's citation by post from his Commanding Officer who added: 'Naturally we are very proud of him, and I know you will be.' It was several weeks later when visiting her in-laws with her two children, in Wesley Street, Cwmbran, that she had the opportunity to show the communication to his proud parents.

It seems ironic that after all the dangerous times 812320 Sergeant John Edwards, 8 Medium Regiment, Royal Artillery, had come through that he should die in a tragic accident in Rangoon. Shortly before the war ended he commenced a new role training army personnel. While instructing a young soldier how to throw a live grenade, the recruit failed to clear the parapet of the throwing bay and the explosion killed both of them. He tragically died on June 27, 1945, age 34 years, and is buried at Rangoon Cemetery, Myanmar.

# HERBERT BAYTON EVANS
**Military Cross**

Born 1923, and the only son of Mr and Mrs
W.J. Evans, Cartref, Stanley Road,
Garndiffaith. An old boy of Garndiffaith and
Abersychan Secondary Schools, he joined the
staff of Messrs E. Nuttall and Co., London. In
January 1943, he proceeded to the Royal
Military College, Sandhurst and later
received a commission before being posted to
the Royal Gloucester Hussars.

He later transferred to an Assault
Squadron of the Royal Engineers and at the
age of twenty-two years was promoted to
Captain in October 1944. In the 12th April
1945 supplement to the *London Gazette* it was
announced that the Military Cross had been
awarded to Captain Herbert Bayton Evans
(288243), Corps of Royal Engineers. The full citation reads:

> *'During an operation on 18/19 January 1945, in the advance to
> Koningsbosch, Captain Bayton-Evans showed great gallantry and
> determination. When mines were encountered in the dark he personally
> controlled the Royal Engineers detachment and supervised the lifting.
> Greatly owing to his determined efforts the column was able to advance
> without any undue delay.*
>
> *On reaching Aanderpopelaar, which was held by the enemy, he requested
> to take part in the attack with his Petard tanks. He advanced on his own
> initiative and blew up the enemy strong points with disregard to enemy
> weapons, SP guns and artillery fire.*
>
> *His determination to overcome all obstacles went a long way towards
> the success of the operation; in fact that operation could not of succeeded
> with a less persistent Officer in charge of the Avre team.'*

Herbert Bayton Evans survived the war and settled in London.

# BRUCE ALASTAIR ROWE-EVANS
## Distinguished Flying Cross

Born November 1921, Bruce Rowe-Evans became the eldest son of Cecil Brankly and Irene Mary Rowe-Evans, of Ponthir. Early schooling took place at St. Dials School, Cwmbran until he won a scholarship to West Monmouthshire Grammar School, Pontypool. Leaving school, he joined the Royal Air Force at the age of fifteen and a half years. As an apprentice on the engineering side, he completed his training by the outbreak of war. With a transfer to flying duties, he received his training in Florida.

In 1941 he married Raymonde, daughter of Mr and Mrs Frank Williams, Weston-super-Mare. They had two sons, David and Richard.

In January 1942 he received his commission and by the end of 1944 his tour of operations concluded. This would coincide with receiving notification of winning the Distinguished Flying Cross. The citation states:

> 'This officer has at all times shown a high degree of courage, skill and initiative.
>
> He has completed a large number of sorties against a wide variety of heavily defended targets as Captain of aircraft.
>
> His cheerful confidence and great ability has inspired a high standard of morale in his crew, who have pressed home all their attacks with the greatest determination.'

Following his discharge from the RAF in 1945 he became a pilot for leading commercial airlines. He died in the mid-1960s and is believed to be buried in the Bahamas.

# HOWARD MILLER EVERETT
### Mentioned in Dispatches

Early in August 1940, a supplement to the London Gazette gave the name of Major Howard M. Everett, of the Royal Monmouthshire Royal Engineers, as mentioned in recognition of 'distinguished services rendered in connection with operations in the field up to March 1940.' He would be mentioned in dispatches not once, but twice during his eventful military career.

Howard M. Everett was the son of Mr. W.J. Everett, the esteemed Pontypool solicitor, and Mrs Everett, of Greenacres, Panteg. He was educated at Uppingham School and Sheffield University before qualifying as a civil engineer. In 1928, the young man wanted to marry, but a slump was on and his finances were low. His father offered him secure employment with his legal firm and, at the age of 33 years, he qualified a second time before joining the Pontypool firm in 1929.

The Panteg man had held a commission in the Royal Artillery at Newport, before joining the Royal Monmouthshire Royal Engineers (Militia) in 1930, and in the same year he obtained his Majority. The issue of a long and happy marriage to Dora Jones, the daughter of Dr. J.H. Jones, Newport, was two sons, Christopher and Robert, and a daughter Jane. Before the war they lived at Windy Ridge, Pontypool.

Major Everett was on a well-deserved leave from France before the evacuation of the British Expeditionary Force in 1940, and on his return became temporary separated from his unit because of the confusion. The Regiments history records:

> 'Major Everett having been sent a very long and slow way round on his way back from leave arrived at Beaumetz-lez-Loges just after the Company had moved and was unable to obtain any information as to where they had gone. Having no form of transport he conducted a large leave party, in the same difficulty, towards the coast by train and on foot and when near Dunkirk was informed that the Company was South of Calais...Major Everett came out on the last boat to leave Calais.'

His second 'Mention' was in June 1945, when he was in charge of the Continental end of PLUTO (Pipe Line Under the Ocean), by which the Forces in their advance on Germany were supplied with petrol from this country. He had 550 men under his command, recruited from various units and trained before D-day. The petrol, after crossing the Channel by under-water pipes to Cherbourg and Boulogne, was pumped many miles inland. Pumping stations erected under huge camouflage nets were to be found at intervals of twenty miles. The saving in transport and fuel was enormous and the Royal Army Service Company never failed to get all the petrol they needed.

To protect the hundreds of miles of pipeline was an almost impossible task and at times placed Lieutenant-Colonel Everett in great danger. Not only did he have to contend with the German threat to the all-important pipeline, but also the local bandits, who would tap into the petrol source and siphon away the fuel. Lieutenant-Colonel Everett always quickly solved these problems by making enquiries as to the sale of petrol on the black market. If there were a surplus of petrol available, at a low price, he would immediately set about locating where the siphoning was taking place.

After the war, Colonel Everett reformed the Royal Monmouthshire Royal Engineers, commanded it from 1948 to 1953, and later succeeded the late Lord Raglan as its Honorary Colonel. He held the Emergency Reserve Decoration, which was awarded him after twenty-six years' service in 1954.

In later life Howard Everett contributed to the community in many helpful ways. He was the founder-president of Pontypool Round Table, a president of the Pontypool Chamber of Trade, and president of Pontypool Theatre Club. He was the right man to take a keen and practical interest in the building and running of Panteg Public Hall, and he and his wife were joint presidents of the New Inn Senior Citizens' Club. As a long-standing member of the Parochial Church Council of St, Mary's Church, Panteg, he designed and made with his own hands a beautiful wooden cross, which still stands in the Garden of Remembrance.

This good man passed away in December 1967 and his ashes were appropriately scattered around the wooden cross he had so tenderly constructed.

# IVOR FORD
## Military Medal

Born June 27, 1916, at Freeholdland, Pontnewynydd, and one of three boys and five girls. His father Alfred worked underground at the Elled Colliery while the eight children, in turn, attended the nearby Snatchwood School. Ivor's first job when leaving school was delivering for Master's Outfitters, Pontypool, but he soon gave up this occupation to become a collier at Llanerch Colliery. At the age of seventeen years he followed his brother to Derby. His brother Alf, a policeman, was a well known boxer who held the middleweight championship of Wales for five years, and then took the light-heavyweight championship. It was from Derby that Ivor was called upon for service in the Territorial Army (3rd Monmouthshire Regiment) on April 11, 1940. His employment at the time of enlistment was a railway shunter.

By 1942, Ivor had met a pretty young lady, one Marie Norvello Cecil, and by special licence they married at Pisgah Baptist Church, Talywain, on April 12, 1942. They would have three boys, Robert, Douglas and Bruce.

As Private (acting Corporal) No. 4080672 Ivor Ford, of the Monmouthshire Regiment, he would be awarded the Military Medal for bravery, near Caen, in October 1944. The official citation states:

> 'On 19th July, Cpl. Ford was Section Corporal with a Mortar Section supporting a company. His job was to relay orders from the Section Commander to the mortar pits. The company came under heavy shell fire as they were clearing the village. Corpl. Ford, seeing a number of casualties, left his slit trench and brought in several wounded men whilst the shell fire was very heavy. In one case he carried a man on his back through a heavy cone whilst at the same time under LMG fire. I consider that he showed complete disregard for his own safety, especially as he was only

*awaiting orders from his section commander. His conduct was a great example to those around at a most critical time.'*

In a letter to his wife at Talywain he wrote: *'Honestly, anyone would have done the same. To my idea everyone ought to have a medal for the great work done there. But there you are, they thought it was a brave deed so they gave me the ribbon. It's nothing to shout about.'* In February 1945, Field Marshal Montgomery pinned the Military Medal on the tunic of Sergeant Ivor Ford in France.

Ivor left the British Amy in January 1946 and returned home to work as a collier in the Blaensychan and Llanerch Collieries. He had boxed for his Division while in the Army and continued to follow the sport. For many years he was a keen and loyal supporter of Pontypool RFC and the remainder of his leisure was thoroughly enjoyed tending his well-kept garden. Every re-union of his regiment would see this brave man in attendance until he passed away on February 5, 1993.

# THOMAS HENRY FURLOW
## Mentioned in Dispatches

Born 5 September, 1909, at Pontypool, the son of Ernest J. Furlow, a master baker, who worked in his brother's bakery at Clarence Corner, Pontypool. With his five brothers he attended Park Street School, Pontypool, and worked for one year underground after completing his education. Although under age, his strong sense of adventure caused him to join the British Army at the age of sixteen years. This decision may have been helped by the fact that his maternal grandfather, Arthur Bessant, served in the Crimea War, and for twenty-one years was drill instructor at Pontypool. His father and two eldest brothers did their duty in World War One. Tom chose to enlist in the Royal Dragoons and it was not very long before his new employers knew his young age. With his regiment about to sail for a tour of duty in India, the young Pontypool lad looked forward to seeing something of the world. Unfortunately, they sailed without him and he narrowly missed having to resign from his new career. However, as soon as he reached the required age, he was sent to join his regiment in India.

While on leave Tom married on Boxing Day, 1936. His young bride was one Edna I. Webb, of Pontypool. The marriage took place at Pontypool Registry Office, but sadly they had no children during the long and happy marriage.

At the outbreak of World War Two, he had completed twelve years service and was a Regimental Sergeant Major with the Royal Dragoons. By this time he had become an expert horseman with the famous regiment. In 1943, R.S.M. T.H. Furlow was mentioned in Dispatches *'for gallant and distinguished service in the Middle East during the period May 1 to October 22, 1942.'* During the period referred to in the dispatch he was wounded in some of the fiercest fighting that marked the Axis retreat in North Africa. Quickly recovering from his wound, the courageous Pontypool man returned to the front and saw the war through.

Tom retired from the army after twenty-six years service. For many years he became the popular landlord of the George Hotel, Pontypool. This occupation was combined with working in an office at Guest, Keen and Nettlefolds, Cwmbran. An accomplished darts player, he organised many keenly fought matches in the district. His love for horses never waned. It would be many years after he had learned his horsemanship with his old regiment that he took great pleasure in teaching his young niece, Shirley Webb, how to ride.

This brave and caring man died February 11 1991, age 81 years.

# THOMAS IVOR GAUNTLETT
### Distinguished Service Medal

Born in 1908, the third son of Mr and Mrs Roger Gauntlett, of 10, Machine Meadow, Freeholdland, Pontnewynydd. Tom Gauntlett attended the local school before enlisting in the Royal Marines in 1926. When only eighteen years of age he became the best marksman among the entire crew of his ship, HMS *Royal Sovereign*, and was presented by the His Majesty with the King's Squad Badge at Olympia, London.

By 1943, he had seen plenty of foreign service and it was while serving on the aircraft carrier *Illustrious* that the thirty-six year old Sergeant would commendably earn the Distinguished Service Medal. The citation tells of Sergeant Gauntlett's '*outstanding coolness and skill in a gallant and successful engagement with a superior force.*'

During his years in the service he married Eunice, a Maltese lady and they had two sons Louis and Robert. After his discharge from the Royal Navy, they lived at Festival Crescent, New Inn, a housing development erected to commemorate the 1951 Festival of Britain. From here he would not have far to travel to his occupation of foreman in the warehouse department at British Nylon Spinners, Pontypool. A brother Leslie was a sapper with the Royal Engineers, and his two other brothers, Albert and George, served with the Colours, until they were recalled to their peacetime occupations as colliers.

This brave man passed away in 1973.

# SIDNEY GRIMISON
## Croix de Guerre

Sidney Grimison came from a family steeped in military tradition. His father had served throughout World War One and his grandfather was in South Africa to witness the Boer War.

Born in 1922, at North Road, Pontypool, and one of four children belonging to Mr and Mrs Sidney Grimison, a tin plate worker. Educated at Town School and Twmpath School, he left to work for a butcher before taking up employment at the Town Forge, Pontypool.

For many years his father had been Quarter Master Sergeant attached to the Panteg Battery, Griffithstown, and, also as a member, young Sid learned the rigors of army life at an early age. This important experience as a territorial would serve him well in the difficult times ahead. He was called up on his eighteenth birthday, in August 1939, and embarked with the Royal Artillery for North West Europe just after D-Day. It would be a long war for the Pontypool forgeman with the only highlight taking place on the day De Gaulle pinned the Croix de Guerre on his chest. His commanding officer wrote the following:

> *'L/Bdr. Grimison's conduct was at all times during the campaign well deserving of the decoration he has received. He spent a great deal of the time at the OP where on many occasions he was under severe and accurate enemy fire, but he never failed to do his job, which was to keep in communication with the guns.'*

After the war Sid worked for Girlings Ltd, Cwmbran and the Civil Service. This quiet and private man never married. Highly regarded by his work colleagues and friends, in later life he became a keen gardener and had a great affection for his dog. He passed away at the age of sixty-three years.

# ELIZABETH MAUD HAMER
### British Empire Medal

Not all the brave deeds during World War Two would occur on distant battlefields and they were most certainly not restricted to just the men of the armed forces. This became a fact when Maud Hamer caught the bus at Pontnewynydd on a cold January morning in 1942. Her thoughts were on the needs of her husband and young children as the bus sped towards Glascoed and she expecting nothing more than to complete her working day helping the war effort.

Born on May 11, 1904, in Griffithstown, near Pontypool, she would have a happy childhood growing up at 2 Spring Terrace, Cwrdy. Her father, Jim Hartland, was in full employment as a tin worker and although times were often hard, he saw to it that his family never went without the basic necessities of life. Maud attended the Griffithstown Council School and returning home on hot summer days she would tarry, like so many others, at the spring near her home. Here, she would quench her thirst with the clear, cold refreshing water, which burst out of the steep mountainside.

When nineteen-years of age, she met, fell in love with, and married William George Hamer, who, like her father, was also a tin worker. The wedding took place on August 6, 1923, at St. Hilda's Church, Griffithstown. Three children would be born to Bill and Maud, a son Clifford, and daughters Dorothy and Barbara.

As the bus approached the Royal Ordnance Factory, Glascoed, Maud's thoughts were for her husband and children and she was already looking forward to spending the evening with her family at their cosy home in Pontnewynydd.

Arriving at the large filling factory, the thirty-seven year old mother reported to her department to commence her checks as a naval examiner and the working day began like so many others. It seemed ages before the time arrived for her to take an official break. As a union representative, it seemed a good opportunity on that fateful morning to visit other departments and collect overdue subscriptions.

As workers continued to fill shells with T.N.T., Maud stepped out into the cold air and had walked but a short distance when a huge explosion ripped apart the area where she had just been standing. Two people lay dead and three others were in a bad way. Had she not decided to attend to her union chores, she would have been lying dead or injured with them. Thick smoke and flames could already be seen coming from the building. Without thought for her own safety, Maud rushed through the smoke and flames to rescue the injured. A man was lying on the floor. Unaided she dragged him into the open air. Remembering her friend, Mrs West, she ran back into the inferno and found her unconscious, hanging from a table. Maud could hardly see because of the fumes, which almost choked her. With great difficulty Mrs West was brought out injured, but still alive. About to enter the burning building a third time her way was barred by worried onlookers who told her that she had done enough.

Maud Hamer luckily suffered no ill effects on that dreadful day and did not think to tell her husband what had happened. It was a few days later when a colleague mentioned the incident and he became aware of his wife's bravery.

For her tremendous courage King George VI presented her with the British Empire Medal at Buckingham Palace. Accompanying her on that memorable day was her husband, son, and daughter Dorothy. Too young to make the trip, her other daughter Barbara would very reluctantly remain at home with her grandmother.

After the war years Bill Hamer moved his family to the new town of Cwmbran and Maud worked for a while in the Pontnewydd Tin Works. Surrounded by lots of friends, she enjoyed the new Bingo entertainment. Never would she be heard to discuss her brave act. Her daughter and son-in-law had been living at her home for over five years when Lenny, rummaging one day in a draw, came across the British Empire Medal. It was not until then that he heard of his mother-in-law's eventful day in 1942.

Elizabeth Maud Hamer spent her last years in the bungalow complex at Sebastopol, near Pontypool. This woman of courage passed away on March 22, 1990, age 84 years.

# WILLIAM PERCY HART
## Military Cross and Mentioned in Dispatches

Born 1909, the only son of Mr James Hart, Bryn Deri, Cwmavon Road, Abersychan, a fireman at Crumlin Valley Colliery. William Percy Hart attended West Monmouthshire School before receiving his theological training at St. Paul's Cathedral, Sussex. He went to Australia in May, 1937, was ordained in Sydney Cathedral the following year and immediately took charge of Bowraville Parish Church, New South Wales.

Early in World War Two the Abersychan padre was Mentioned in Dispatches for gallant conduct during the evacuation of Greece, where he served with the Australians. During this action he was slightly wounded when his ship was torpedoed. He would again show signs of tremendous bravery during a ferocious engagement with Japanese forces in New Guinea. In October 1942, his further bravery earned him the Military Cross for gallantry. The Japanese were strongly attacking an Australian unit, and a number of men had been wounded. Captain Hart and some of his comrades went out to within fifty yards of the enemy position and took back the wounded to safety. The official citation reads:

> 'On October 26th, 1942, at Eora Creek, New Guinea, Captain Hart, who was attached to the Regimental Aid Post, led a stretcher party on an arduous hill climb to a detached position. Despite the fact that the line of communication was under heavy fire from an enemy position fifty yards distant, he successfully bypassed the position. His fearless leadership, personal courage and complete disregard for his own safety were an inspiration to the men, and led to the successful evacuation of the casualties. Later, on October 27th, 1942, when the Regimental Aid Post came under heavy mountain fire, Captain Hart was again an inspiration to both orderlies and patients. Despite heavy fire he arranged shelters for wounded cases, and with a cheery smile gave them confidence. On many occasions he fearlessly assisted wounded men in. Throughout the campaign he continued to inspire the men and was a considerable force in maintaining the morale of the unit at a high standard.'

In 1943, William Percy Hart married an Australian nurse and after the war they made their home in Sydney, Australia.

# CECIL A. HEAD
### Distinguished Service Cross

Born 1912, the only son of Mabel and Henry Harold Head, 37 Park Street, Blaenavon. Mr Head became a dispenser to Blaenavon Medical Society for many years. Cecil Head was educated at West Monmouthshire School and continued with a scholarship to Jesus College, Oxford, where he graduated BA and later MA. Before the outbreak of World War II he was a master at King's School, Rochester.

By 1943, Lieutenant Cecil Head, Royal Navy Volunteer Reserve, was in command of a motor launch, belonging to a flotilla of the same vessels, which went out to the Mediterranean in March that year and for about three months did anti-submarine patrols off the Algerian coast. Around this time the six motor launches, which made up the flotilla, landed American forces who captured Ventotene Island, some thirty-five miles west of Naples, and three hours before the landing at Salerno. On board a motor launch they had Lieutenant Douglas Fairbanks, of the U.S. Navy, and an American war correspondent, John Steinbeck, the playwright. Then they took part in the invasion of Sicily. Two days and nights were spent at sea during the operation and the weather was very bad. This was followed by fourteen days operating off the beaches, making smoke screens, patrolling, acting as escorts and doing all manner of jobs. It was during this action that the Blaenavon man had to use all his manoeuvring skills. Six enemy aircraft made a determined attack on his motor launch. They swooped down while machine gunning his launch, but he got away unscathed and shot them up considerably. After that the flotilla went back to escorting convoys.

Later, Lieutenant Cecil Head, RNVR, earned the award of the Distinguished Service Cross for gallantry, skill and devotion to duty shown in the operations which led to the successful landing of Allied forces in the south of France.

Cecil Head survived the war and returned to the teaching profession.

# BENJAMIN WILLIAM HILL
## Distinguished Flying Medal

Born 1922 at Blaenavon, Monmouthshire. His father George Hill served in the 1914-18 war with the Royal Welsh Fusiliers on the North-west Frontier of India and between the wars he was employed at Corbie by the War Graves Commission. The Hill family continued to live at King Street, Blaenavon and young Ben attended the local schools. With his education completed Ben Hill joined his father working for the War Graves Commission and was in France when war broke out. He was fortunate to be evacuated from Dunkirk.

It did not take the young Blaenavon man long to join up and go on active service. As a Flight Sergeant in the Royal Air Force, he took part in thirty operational flights over enemy territory by 1944. In March of the same year he married Miss Myra Workman, a twin daughter of Mr and Mrs W. Workman, who owned a family butchers shop in Broad Street, Blaenavon. Flight Sergeant Hill and A/CW1 Myra Workman, WAAF, married by special licence in Broad Street Methodist Church, Blaenavon. In June 1944, he was awarded the Distinguished Flying Medal for courage and devotion to duty.

King George VI presented Flight Sergeant Hill with his medal at an investiture in Buckingham Palace. With him on the special day was his mother, father and mother-in-law, Mrs W. Workman.

Warrant Officer B.W. Hill, DFM, survived the war and continued to be employed by the War Graves Commission for many years.

# WILLIAM HOLVEY
## Certificate of Good Service

A framed Certificate of Good Service signed by Field Marshall Montgomery would deservedly hang on the wall in the home of Lance Corporal William Holvey for many years. Born in Blaenavon on November 18, 1909, he left school to follow his father down the pit.

Around 1927 he joined the Welsh Guards and while on leave in London in 1932, a chance meeting with a Ferndale girl changed his life. Gwendoline Harris was in domestic service in the capital city and they were to marry the following year in Pontypridd Registry Office. He completed his contract with the British Army and returned to the Blaenavon collieries. Two children would result from the happy union, Joan Mary Florence, the first born, and a son Anthony.

As a reservist, just prior to the outbreak of war he was called up. Bill had a choice to either stay down the pit or serve his country. Without hesitation he re-joined the Welsh Guards. Difficult times were to be witnessed by the young Blaenavon man in France and Belgium before the collapse of the two nations. He would never forget the evacuation of Dunkirk. He again landed on French soil on D-Day and as a foot soldier and dispatch rider, accompanied his regiment all the way to Germany.

In 1945 he was awarded the Certificate of Good Service, which said:

> '*It has been brought to my notice that you have performed outstanding good service, and shown great devotion to duty, during the campaign in France.*
> *I award you this certificate as a token of my appreciation, and I have given instructions that this shall be noted in your Record of Service.*'
>
> > *B.L. Montgomery,*
> > *Field Marshall,*
> > *Commander-in-Chief,*
> > *21st Army Group.*

After the war Bill Holvey again became a collier for a time and then worked at the Blaenavon tyre mill. He completed his working life at Girlings Limited, Cwmbran. Bill had been a successful athlete in the Army and continued to enjoy the local sports scene. A period as chairman of the local Comrades Club would be a proud time in later life. Always known for his good work, Bill Holvey died on 12 January 1989.

# RONALD LENNARD HOOPER
## Distinguished Flying Medal

Born Cairo, January 29, 1917. His father was one Frederick Joseph Hooper, who married Evelyn Lavinia Lennard, formerly of 'The Laurels,' Station Road, Pontnewydd, Cwmbran. They had two boys, Peter the eldest, and Ronald. A well-paid post with Maspero Freres, a Danish tobacco company, had taken F.J. Hooper to Cairo and it was here that his youngest son spent the first two years of his life. Mrs Hooper returned from abroad to live at her parent's home 'The Laurels' Pontnewydd, (now the British Legion headquarters). It was here young Ronald grew up while first attending the local school and later the West Monmouthshire School, Pontypool. On leaving school he worked for Bunning & Russell, Estate Agents and Auctioneers, at Pontypool. He enjoyed sport, playing

rugby and cricket for local teams. During this period he met his future wife who was a member of the clerical staff of the Pontnewydd Tin Stamping Works.

In 1939, Ronald L. Hooper joined the Royal Air Force as an air gunner and subsequently completed a large number of operational flights against targets as a member of the Pathfinder bomber crews, the men who blazed a trail for their comrades to follow. His was one of the most hazardous jobs in the R.A.F. and the life expectancy for each crew was very low. Early in his service he experienced two crashes when returning in badly damaged planes from raids on enemy territory.

During leave, on June 6, 1942, Ronald Hooper married his fiancé Miss Laura Gregory, of Rockhill Road, Pontypool. The wedding took place at St. James' Church, Pontypool, and the issue of the happy union was a beautiful baby girl, which they named Ann.

In August 1943, Flight Sergeant Hooper was based at Gravely, Huntingdonshire with No. 35 Pathfinder squadron and had done over fifty operational flights. On August 16/17 1943, he was shot down over Turin, Italy, on his fifty seventh operational flight. Only two were able to escape by parachute from the burning plane. Ron Hooper was the second to leave. He broke his shoulder blade on landing and when captured was taken to an Italian military hospital for treatment. Later, he was moved to Germany and spent the next few years in various Prisoner of War camps before returning home in May 1945.

Almost to the day it was announced Flight Sergeant R.L. Hooper had been awarded the Distinguished Flying Medal, news reached his wife at Pontypool informing her that her husband was missing after an operational flight. Had he completed sixty operational flights, he would have had a spell on ground staff as an instructor. It was an agonizing four weeks before she heard he was safe and a prisoner of war in Italy.

With the war over Warrant Officer Ronald L. Hooper, and his wife Laura, visited Buckingham Palace where he was invested by the King with the Distinguished Flying Medal. His citation reads:

> *'Sergeant Hooper has taken part, as wireless operator, in a large number of night operational flights against the enemy. He has completed operational missions against such targets as Cologne, Duisburg, Essen, and Dortmund, and during his first tour of duty attacked many objectives in the Middle East. Sergeant Hooper has, by his technical skill and personal qualities, played an important part in the success of his crew.'*

With the war over Ron Hooper, DFM, resided at Usk Road, Pontypool, and after a short spell with an insurance company, he joined British Nylon Spinners (ICI Fibres) in 1948, commencing as a process worker. Obtaining promotion within a few years, he had a successful career with the company as a Works Study Engineer until his retirement in 1978.

Always a very keen supporter of Pontypool RFC, his remaining leisure time was taken up with reading, writing, music and walking. This brave man passed away on February 9, 1979.

# ALBERT JOHN HORTON
**Distinguished Flying Cross**

Charles Horton came over from Risca in search of work and fortunately found regular employment as a roll turner at Avondale Tinplate Works. His son John was born on February 23, 1922, at the family home in Pontnewydd, and he grew up to serve his country well during the dark days of the Second World War. John first attended Pontnewydd Endowed School and later the West Monmouthshire School, Pontypool, prior to entry to Clark's Commercial College. His first job was for the Monmouthshire County Council, at County Hall, Newport, and this proved to be the beginning of a long career as a civil servant.

The young Pontnewydd man enlisted for aircrew in 1941, trained in Canada and was commissioned in 1943. From 1943 he became a valued member of 115 Squadron and flew regularly in Lancaster II bombers. An entry in the *London Gazette* gave witness to Pontnewydd folk that the popular local man had been awarded the Distinguished Flying Cross. The citation states:

> '*The King has been pleased to approve the following award in recognition of gallantry and devotion to duty in the execution of air operations:*
>
> *D.F.C. – Pilot Officer Albert John Horton, 170875 Royal Air Force Volunteer Reserve, No. 115 Squadron.*
>
> *Pilot Officer Horton has completed a large number of sorties as bomb aimer, many of them being attacks on distant and dangerous targets in Germany. During one mission to Hanover, his aircraft was attacked by enemy night fighters before reaching the target. The rear gunner was killed and two of the crew injured. Pilot Officer Horton gave his captain valuable assistance on this occasion, helping him to control the badly damaged aircraft and to fly it to safe landing at base. He has always shown outstanding ability and a strong sense of duty.*'

After the war John returned to work at the County Hall, Newport. He has three children, Ruth, Neil and Carl. Retired and residing in Newport, leisure time is taken up with gardening and following sport. He is particularly proud to be chairman of Gwent Pre-retirement Council and is on the board of the YMCA.

# MAXWELL HORTON
### Mentioned in Dispatches

Born June 5, 1920, at the family home Pontnewydd, the son of Charles Horton, roll turner at Avondale Tinplate Works. The elder of two boys, he first attended Pontnewydd Endowed School and later the West Monmouthshire School, Pontypool. Before enlisting in 1939 he was on the clerical staff in the Surveyor's Department of the Monmouthshire County Council.

In a souvenir brochure describing the exploits of 531 Field Battery, Royal Artillery, the name Captain Horton twice appears for special mention. First, during action in the Siegfried Line, when he and another officer showed themselves time and again to heavy fire in successful efforts to get observation and send down accurate fire orders, and later, on the Elbe, when Lieutenant Horton and a colleague accompanied the assaulting infantry and had to carry their wireless sets up a 200-foot cliff while exposed to sniper fire.

After the war Max attended a teaching course at Burderop Park Training College, Wiltshire, and later obtained a special Diploma at Carnegie Physical Education College, Leeds. The young man was delighted to return and teach in his old school at Pontypool.

While playing tennis Max met Miss Joan Davey, a chemistry mistress employed at Pontypool County School for Girls, and they married at Griffithstown Baptist Church in August 1952. Best man was Mr John Horton, DFC, brother of the bridegroom. The issue of the happy union was a baby girl Sally Anne, born on January 13, 1959, at Panteg Maternity Hospital. Later they would enjoy the company of three grandsons, Daniel, Nicholas and Patrick.

Max always thoroughly enjoyed sport. He played football for Newport County AFC and captained Pontypool RFC from 1948 to 1950, and also captained a Welsh trial team. He was one of the finest outside-halves in Wales and only one man kept him out of the national side, the legendary Billy Cleaver. He did get to sit on the subs' bench but was desperately unlucky never to win a cap.

Maxwell Horton was a long serving member of West Monmouthshire Comprehensive School and esteemed and much loved by generations of pupils. He was a tireless worker for the church and had been a deacon at Richmond Road Church, Pontnewydd, for around fifty years. This Christian gentleman of Sunnybank Way, Griffithstown, passed away on May 13 1999, age 78 years.

# MARY HUGHES
### Certificate of Merit

Born December 15, 1919, at Cardiff, the first child of Frank and Jesse Hughes. Frank Hughes was a director of Henry Hughes Newspapers Ltd., proprietors of the *Free Press of Monmouthshire* and had been on active service in the First World War. He returned to Pontypool after the war and remained with the popular newspaper until his death. Her mother, (then Jesse Palmer Morgan), qualified as a State Registered Nurse at Pontypool Hospital and was Assistant Matron in the mobile Welsh Field Hospital in France. For her huge contribution during the Great War she received the coveted Royal Red Cross Medal and was also decorated by the French War Office.

Mary obviously came from good stock. Educated at Mount Pleasant School, Pontypool Convent School and Pontypool Girls' County School, after which she stayed at home to look after her invalid mother. A month after her mother's death, in 1941, she joined the First Aid Nursing Yeomanry as an ambulance driver and continued to act in that capacity in the ATS throughout the Second World War.

Mary was stationed all around South Wales, including Newport, Swansea and Manobier in Pembrokeshire. In September 1943, the young Pontypool woman would show remarkable courage while dealing with an incendiary bomb, which fell on the petrol store attached to a hospital during a blitz on a west coast town. For her bravery she deservedly received a Certificate of Merit.

The incendiary bomb had a warhead of magnesium, which burned so hot that it could melt through steel. Mary had been trained to deal with this kind of weapon and realised that she had to act quickly before it passed through the roof of the petrol store and the whole district would be devastated. While her colleagues dealt with the easily accessible bombs, Mary grabbed some sandbags and quickly climbed onto the roof of the petrol store. The deadly device was already doing its work, but with seconds to spare, Mary correctly placed the sandbags and prevented the bomb from receiving the oxygen necessary for it to complete its dastardly act. In the years that followed Mary modestly told people that after routinely cleaning the ambulances she became so annoyed with the German aircraft for disrupting her work and felt that something had to be done - but there should be no doubt, this was a act of great bravery and similar actions had earned a far higher award.

Mary spent the rest of the war driving ambulances, staff cars and riding military motorcycles. By the end of the war she had acquired a dog, 'Skipper' a border

collie. He was also a keen motorcyclist sitting between Mary and the fuel tank. He was demobilised with her from the ATS in 1945. Skipper was the first in a long line of dogs that accompanied her throughout her life. She became an ardent animal lover, passionately opposed to any form of animal cruelty.

She returned to Pontypool after the war and must have found it difficult to get back into the routine of everyday life. Like many women of her time, she had no formal job or profession and so went back to running her father's house in Penygarn.

It would not be long before Mary met, fell in love, and married Llewellyn Williams, an employee of Lloyd's Bank, Pontypool. Initially from Abercrave, in the Swansea Valley, he moved around the banks' branches in South Wales as he ascended the management ladder. They were married in 1949 and the issue of the happy union was a son Huw, born at Cefn Ila Hospital, Usk, in 1951.

Her son did her proud. In 1970 he went to St Mary's Hospital Medical School, London, and qualified in 1976. He became a General Practitioner in Trowbridge, Wiltshire, in 1981, and has been there ever since. Mary was very proud of her four grandchildren and they were undoubtedly one of the most special things in her life. This lady of rare and unyielding courage died on Boxing Day 1989.

# WILLIAM HERBERT IRVING
### Distinguished Flying Cross

It is a feeling that greater things were to come from Wing Commander William I. Irving, DFC, who sadly lost his life in the 1950 Welsh air disaster.

Born December 10, 1918, Bill Irving became the youngest son of Mr and Mrs T.R. Irving, 'Croydon,' Edward Street, Griffithstown, near Pontypool. Early schooling took place at Griffithstown Mixed School and West Monmouthshire School. Further education at the Technical College, Crumlin, accompanied his apprentiship with the South Wales Electric Power Company, Cwmbran, before the commencement of World War Two.

In June 1939, he joined the Royal Artillery and within three months received a commission. An early introduction to the great dangers of war occurred in France, just before that country capitulated. As part of a Search-light Battery, he was fortunate to be evacuated from Dunkirk with only fifty of his Battery of seventy-five men surviving. He would later tell of his escape to England in a rowing boat.

In May 1941, he transferred to the Royal Air Force and got his 'wings' in just six months. It was a busy time for the young Griffithstown man while attached to various operational stations in Britain and North Africa.

On December 4th, 1942, he took part in a flight of light bombers, which has become legend. His Wing-Commander Hugh G. Malcolm, having been detailed to give close support to the First Army, received an urgent request to attack an enemy fighter airfield near Cheuigui. He knew that to attack such an objective without a fighter escort – which could not be arranged in time – would be to court almost certain disaster. But, with the knowledge that hundreds of lives of allied troops would certainly be lost if the airfield was not destroyed, he took off with his squadron. Things went well on the flight to the target, but when his squadron had successfully attacked, an overwhelming force of enemy fighters attacked them.

Wing Commander Malcom fought back, controlling his hard-pressed squadron and attempting to maintain formation. One by one his squadron was shot down, until only his own aircraft remained. In the end he, too, was shot down in flames. Flight Lieutenant Irving's crew was the only one to escape with their lives; they successfully baled out and walked back to base. Wing Commander Malcolm received the Victoria Cross posthumously for his bravery and determination on that eventful day.

While on leave, Flight Lieutenant Irving met and fell in love with a young Cwmbran woman. In September 1943, he married Miss Hazel Rees of Llantarnam Road, Cwmbran and a son Robin was born the following year.

The war was far from over for the Griffithstown man. He would take part in many operational flights flying various aircrafts. On D-Day he had a lucky escape when struck by enemy fire, smoke filled the cockpit causing temporary damage to his eyes. Using all his flying skill he brought the plane home. Later he would fly in three of the 1000 bomber raids over Germany. By April 1945, Squadron Leader Irving, in addition to being a fine leader and a fearless captain on operations, had done much to inspire with confidence the less experienced crews in his flight and maintain their morale at a high level. For his huge contribution he was awarded the Distinguished Flying Cross. The particulars of meritorious service for which the recommendation was made are:

> 'Squadron Leader Irving, as Captain and Pilot of bomber aircraft has completed two tours of operations – the first in the Middle East and the second on Lancaster aircraft against such targets as Dijon, Caen, Brunswick, and Duisburg in France and Germany.
>
> He acted as Flight Commander throughout his second tour with Nos. 100 and 626 Squadrons, mostly at the former where he did excellent work and was of great assistance to the Squadron Commander. He proved himself to be a first class operational pilot and his skill and offensive spirit won the respect of his crew and his flight. He did much to assist in the running of the Squadron and gave valuable support at a time when it was most needed.
>
> For his work and the satisfactory results achieved by his flight I recommend that this Officer be awarded the Distinguished Flying Cross.'

After the war Bill Irving rejoined the staff of the South Wales Electricity Board and remained in touch with Llandow Airfield. His leisure time was taken up as a member of St. Hilda's Church choir and participating in various local sporting events. He played cricket for Panteg C.C., rugby, and particularly enjoyed horse riding. A proud moment in his life was when he received notification that he had been chosen to represent Wales at hockey.

In November 1946, it became known that Squadron Leader William H. Irving would command the recently reformed 614 (County of Glamorgan) Auxiliary Squadron based at Llandow Airfield. Through this part-time post he became a tremendous asset in the recruitment of young men to a career in the Royal Air Force.

It would be a black day in the history of the eastern valley of Monmouthshire when a chartered flight of rugby supporters, returning from an International match in Ireland, crashed, when approaching Llandow airfield. Thirteen local men died that day, among them Squadron Leader William H. Irving, DFC. It seems ironic that this good man who still had so much to offer the community, and humanity as a whole, and who had come through the nightmare of World War Two, should pass into history in such a moving way.

Appropriately, Bill Irving's ashes was scattered from an aircraft over Llandow airfield, a place he loved and had given so much of himself. He was a truly brave man in all ways and the memorial windows still to be seen at St. Hilda's Church, Griffithstown, are testimony to this.

# HENRY BERNARD ISRAEL
## Mentioned in Dispatches

The Germans were advancing down the pass in great numbers. Overwhelmed, the British officer ordered his men to withdraw. Gunner H.B. Israel's gun covered the hasty retreat. Several times his officer called to him to come away, but each time he replied, "Just another round, Sir." His gun was the last to withdraw and undoubtedly gave his comrades the opportunity to reach safety. For his bravery and tenacity Bernard Israel would be Mentioned in Dispatches and receive the coveted Oak Leaf.

Bernard was born in Blaenavon while his father toiled in the depths of Big Pit Colliery. His passion for the game of rugby surfaced while playing for Hillside School. He later played regularly for the 'Quins' at scrum-half and often helped out the town's premiere side. His first job after leaving school was for the Blaenafon Co-op, but they would not allow him time off on a Saturday afternoon to play rugby. This situation caused him to become a collier and made it possible to throw the oval ball about every week-end.

On June 6 1939, and almost twenty-one years of age, he enlisted in the British Army. After training at Woolwich, time was spent in India before seeing action in Egypt. Almost immediately he was in the thick of the fighting as a gun layer in the first attack on Sidi Barranni with the Indian 4th Division. Wounded by shrapnel in the leg at Tobruk, he was unlucky when the Germans captured the ambulance taking him to hospital. Nothing would be heard of Bernard for some time and he was posted as 'missing.'

The former 'Quins' scrumhalf had become a prisoner in an Italian camp. Despite being well treated by the Italian guards he was determined to escape. With Arthur Price, another Blaenavon man, he escaped and joined a Partisan group. He had heard a rumour about being 'Mentioned' just before his capture, but events had moved along so dramatically that the possibility of the special honour was forgotten. From the 8th September 1943 until the liberation the two Blaenavon men fought with the Partisans and Bernard received their special medal and a certificate.

Because of a leg injury Bernard left the army in 1946. Unknown to him, his mother had died while he was away. While waiting to catch a bus in Newport to his home, the news was broken to him by the driver, a distant relative by marriage. It would be twelve months after being demobilised that ex-gunner Israel was officially notified that he had been 'Mentioned in Dispatches.' He returned to his work as a collier and continued to play rugby. Today, he lives happily with his wife in Rhydynos Street, Blaenavon and has two daughters, Lorraine who lives in Australia and Patricia.

# JESSE WATKINS JENKINS
## Certificate of Commendation

Jesse Watkins Jenkins grew up in Blaenavon and was well thought of by all he came into contact with. The son of Mr and Mrs A. Jenkins, 25 Phillip Street, he attended the town's schools before taking up employment at the Blaenavon branch of Messrs Liptons'.

Following his call up he spent five years with the Royal Artillery and as an anti-aircraft gunner, was on duty at Cardiff and Swansea during the height of the blitz. He landed in France on D-Day. In January 1945, he received a Certificate of Commendation for gallantry in the field: *'At the risk of his own life, Gunner Jenkins went into a minefield to render first aid to a seriously wounded soldier with the result that the man's life was saved.'*

While on leave in July 1945, Jesse married a local girl at Park Street Methodist Church before returning to active service with the Liberation Army. It was only four months later that his wife received the dreaded telegram to say that Jesse had been killed under circumstances unknown.

1582346 Gunner Jesse Watkins Jenkins, 363 Battery, 112 H.A.A. Regiment, was laid to rest quietly at a lovely, well-tended cemetery at Putzchen, near the Rhine. A friend placed roses on the grave for his wife. The grave was later re-located to the large Cologne Southern Cemetery. The name of the brave young man can be seen on the Blaenavon War Memorial.

# SYLVESTER ROBERT JOLLIFFE
### Mentioned in Dispatches

It was a cold, windy morning when the communication dropped through the letterbox of 7, Prince Street, Pontypool. The news was good and Mrs Jolliffe waited eagerly for her husband, Harold, to return home from his work as a collier at one of the many pits found in the valley. The letter, received from their youngest son, Stoker 1st Class Sylvester Robert Jolliffe, told that he had been Mentioned in Dispatches for energy and devotion to duty during the Sicilian campaign and landings on the Italian mainland.

Bob Jolliffe was born at Ivy Farm, at the bottom of Broadway, Pontypool, on 23, June 1923. With his sister and brother he attended George Street, School and later would have been found working as a collier, or in the Pontypool Town Forge. With his older brother Stan serving in the RAF, Bob decided early in 1942 to join the Royal Navy. He served for four years.

At the time of receiving his 'Mention in Dispatches' on 25th January 1944, he was employed on assault crafts under an officer for who he had tremendous respect. On one occasion SAS commandos were landed with the purpose of capturing a nearby viaduct in readiness for the tanks to come up. Bob's assault craft became exposed to great danger as they waited off shore for the time to collect the raiding party when their job was done. Towards the end of the war in Europe it became necessary for him to attend a course in preparation for transfer to Japanese waters, but after four years continuous service he decided to leave the Navy on a job release scheme. This allowed men to be released to go back to vital occupations and the fit young man returned to work in the colliery.

On March 26th, 1951, the marriage took place at the All Trinity Church, Pontnewydd, of Bob Jolliffe and Marjorie Joyce Crockett, a local girl. A son Phillip and three grandchildren would be the result of the happy event.

Bob Jolliffe enjoyed life to the full. His love of rugby would fill the winter months while two large garden allotments kept him fit for many years. Well known for his champion pigeons, his fine tenor voice would add to his fame and be made available for any good cause. The remaining eighteen years of his working life was in a deservedly lighter occupation at the Royal Ordnance Factory, Glascoed. Visitors to 11 Upper Park Terrace, Pontypool still receive a warm welcome before enjoying Bob's irrepressible sense of humour.

# COLIN REES JONES
**Distinguished Service Cross**

Born 1914, the only son of Mr Rees Jones, headmaster of Blaenavon Endowed Boys' School. He was educated at Blaenavon Endowed Boys' School, West Monmouthshire School, and St Mary's College, Cheltenham. He became vice-captain of West Monmouthshire rugby team and captain of Cheltenham. A keen musician from an early age, he later served as organist at the parish church Folkestone, where he was headmaster of a school before joining up. He joined the Royal Navy Volunteer Reserve as an ordinary seaman and served for a long period in the cruiser *Eurylaus*. Thirty years of age and married with one son, Lieutenant Jones won the Distinguished Service Cross for extremely dangerous work on the beaches of Salerno. The May 19, 1944, edition of the *London Gazette* gave notice that Temporary Sub-Lieutenant Colin Rees Jones, R.N.V.R., had won the prestigious award.

Colin Rees Jones, DSC, survived the war and returned to the teaching profession.

# EDWIN LLEWELLYN JONES
## Certificate for Good Service

Born April 26, 1906, in the Pontypool district, the son of Edwin Jones, collier, and his wife Amelia. Edwin had a brother Ivor and three sisters, Sylvia, Edith and Gwyneth, and all attended the local schools. After leaving school he joined his father who was working in a nearby colliery. On December 24th, 1932, he married Edna May Dix, of Pontypool, and the happy event occurred in the parish church Trevethin. Their home would be at 7, School View, Pontymoile, near Pontypool, and no children were the outcome of the marriage.

Edwin joined the British Army on March 13, 1941, and served continuously until his discharge in Hamburg, Germany, on February 12, 1946. Since 1934, he had been a keen member of the St. John Ambulance Brigade and this skill was of tremendous value to the Army. Gunner Jones acted as a medical orderly to his Heavy Anti Aircraft Unit, which landed on the Normandy beaches on D-plus 4 Day. Exactly a month later, during the heavy fighting behind Caen, three of his comrades were badly wounded by a shell, which fell among them. Gunner Jones immediately rendered first aid and his knowledge undoubtedly saved lives. At the appropriate time he evacuated them from the dangerous area.

Expressing his appreciation of Gunner Jones's work, the Battalion Commander stated in Orders:

> 'By his ceaseless and untiring efforts he displayed not only great devotion to his comrades, but a coolness in emergency that did much to assist in every way possible. His work merits the highest possible praise.'

Edwin returned from the war to work for many years at Panteg Steelworks. In this heavy industry his job was that of a de-scaler, removing the outer impurities from the heated ingots. He continued his work for the St. John's Ambulance Brigade and with time reached the senior position of Superintendent. A quiet man of strong religious conviction, he attended the Pontymoile Mission Church for most of his life. A long spell at the church as a Sunday School teacher coincided with an enjoyable time as a choir member.

This brave and caring man passed away January 24, 1969, age 62 years.

# WILLIAM LESLIE JONES
**Mentioned in Dispatches**

Born August 30, 1917, at Wainfelin, Pontypool. His father, Hopkin Jones, lived at Brynwern and had been a 'roller' in Town Forge for many years. With his two brothers, Les attended George Street School, Pontypool, before commencing work in a shoe shop in the small town. At the outbreak of war the young man joined up and served in the Royal Engineers throughout its duration. It was while home on leave he courted Winifred Dodge, of Pontypool, and after requesting fourteen days special leave the couple married at St. James' Church. Two daughters, Barbara and Janet, were the issue of the happy marriage.

As the war progressed Les gained promotion to Lance Sergeant. As a member of a bomb disposal unit, he assisted in many dangerous tasks after enemy bombing of coastal towns and abroad. After some particularly dangerous work the name of Lance Sergeant W.L. Jones, Royal Engineers, was published in the *London Gazette* on March 22, 1945 for being Mentioned in Dispatches

After six years Les was demobilised and returned to his former occupation in the Pontypool shoe shop. Later he worked for many years at ICI, Mamhilad. He enjoyed following local sport and was a warden at St. James' Church, Pontypool. He served the local church well for over forty-five years. A former member of the British Legion, in his younger days he regularly attended the Armistice Day parade and on occasions he laid the wreath at the Pontypool War Memorial.

Today, Les is a sprightly eighty-six years old and remains a perfect gentleman.

# AUBREY KNIGHT
## Commended for Gallantry

Born 1920, the youngest son of Thomas and Rachel Knight. Before World War II Aubrey lived at his parent's home in Snatchwood Road, Abersychan, and worked for his brother, Mr. Ron Knight, a well-known fruiterer and greengrocer, who had business interests in Pontypool, Griffithstown and Pontnewydd. Later he worked at a local factory as a lorry driver and gradually took an interest in the haulage trade. Although his health was generally in a poor state he was determined to join the Army in August 1940, and became a driver in the Royal Army Service Corps.

While on home leave, the quiet young man met Mary Pauling, the third daughter of Mr and Mrs W. Pauling of Alexandra Road, Sebastopol, Monmouthshire. Their marriage was solemnised on June 27, 1942, at St. Hilda's Church, Griffithstown. A son Noel would be born to the happy couple on Christmas Day, 1950.

In October 1942, while working at his depot, the shy Abersychan man had no reason to believe that his day would be any different to the others that he had spent in the quiet part of the English countryside. Suddenly, nearby, an aircraft came from somewhere and crashed not far from where he was standing. Without thought for his own safety he dashed to the wrecked plane, which was burning fiercely. He cut the unconscious pilot's straps and dragged him clear within seconds of the aircraft becoming a ball of flame.

Describing the prompt and courageous behaviour of the twenty-two year as 'outstanding,' the Police Superintendent of the Division in which the plane crashed wrote the following to driver Knights Commanding Officer:

> 'Driver Knight was the first person on the scene when the aircraft crashed, and with great presence of mind and showing the utmost coolness and courage, he dragged the unconscious pilot out of the burning plane and carried him to safety. The pilot's clothing was on fire when Knight got him clear of the plane. I think his prompt action is deserving of the highest praise. Although he did everything humanely possible to save the life of the pilot, he succumbed to his multiple injuries. Nevertheless, his conduct on this occasion is a credit to his unit and the Army generally, and it is with pleasure that I bring it to your notice.'

The G.O.C. – in – Chief, Western Command, in due course commended Lance Corporal Aubrey Knight, R.A.S.C., in orders.

Aubrey was later discharged from the Army and lived at Hill Street Griffithstown, near Pontypool. He entered into partnership with his brother Harold and for a while managed a successful haulage business. Sadly, with his son about to celebrate a sixth birthday on Christmas Day 1956, this brave man died after a long illness on December 21. He was 36 years of age.

# WILLIAM ALFRED LIAS
**Military Medal**

On May 7, 1918, a son was born to Alfred and Ann Lias, of Cwmffrwdoer, Pontypool. With his six brothers and sister, he attended Pontnewynydd School while his father toiled as a collier in the nearby coal mine. At the age of thirteen years he left school and joined his father down the pit.

With the outbreak of war Bill Lias joined the 2/4th Battalion, The Hampshire Regiment, and saw action in North Africa, Italy, Greece and France. During the final battle of Cassino, Private Lias earned the Military Medal for extreme bravery. The mountain terrain was so rugged that the supplies and ammunition he organised could only be transported on the backs of mules. It was while on a mountain track along a ledge, which looked down into a deep gully, that a halt was called so that the mules could be rested. The ammunition had just been unloaded and piled neatly when the party was suddenly ambushed. Trapped, finding what little cover possible became a priority. Unable to move either backwards or forwards, another even more dangerous situation became apparent when it was seen that the boxes of ammunition had been hit and caught fire. Quickly realising that everyone on the narrow ledge would be killed when the ammunition exploded, he ran forward. Exposing himself to enemy fire, Private Lias jumped up on the pile of ammunition and proceeded to throw the burning boxes over the side of the ledge. There would be huge explosions as they fell into the gully. With the immediate danger almost over he was unfortunate that the last box of ammunition exploded not long after it had left his hands. With many shrapnel wounds, he was lucky to survive. The official recording of the action for which he was commended states:

> 'On the night of 16/17 April 1944 the mortar platoon, of which Private Lias is a mortar detachment member, was in action shooting a DF task.
>
> The platoon came under heavy shelling and a dump of mortar bombs was set on fire.
>
> With great presence of mind and disregard for self, Private Lias rushed to the burning dump and endeavoured to put out the fire with his leather jerkin.

*Failing to control the blaze, he immediately started to scatter the bombs. By this time, on account of the glow, the enemy opened on the dump with MG fire. In spite of this, Private Lias still continued to scatter the ammunition, until he was wounded by the exploding bombs. His action not only set a very high standard of courage, but also saved the nearby mortar crew from casualties, and enabled them to continue firing their DF task, which was vital at that time.'*

He could have returned home, but made a terrific effort to get fit and returned to duty. Due to difficult circumstances, the medal, with the King's certificate, was received without ceremony while in Italy.

While on leave Bill Lias met a pretty WAAF at a local dance hall. He married Violet Prince, from Abercarn, at Pontypool, in December 1947. After the war Bill worked at collieries in the Pontypool district and finally at West End Colliery, Abercarn. They had three children, Raymonde, Malcolm and Janet. Always a popular member of the Pantside Club, Newbridge, he and his wife kept up their interest in dancing and his children remember how their parents would, without fail, attend a dance together every Saturday night.

This brave man of the valleys died in 2002 at the age of 84 years.

# ALFRED JOHN LLOYD
## Military Medal

Born 1922, the youngest son of Major and Gwendoline Lloyd, of Picton Street, Griffithstown, Monmouthshire. With his elder brother Hubert and sister Phyllis, he attended the Griffithstown Mixed Council School before working for a while as a porter at Pontypool Road Railway Station. At the outbreak of war Jack trained up as a gunner at Leith, Edinburgh.

Gunner Lloyd would undoubtedly have an adventurous life. Early in his military service he was Mentioned in Dispatches and awarded the Oak Leaf for saving the life of a seaman in the shark infested waters of the Atlantic Ocean. While serving as a gunner attached to the Merchant Navy, he won the Military Medal for devotion to duty when the military ammunition ship in which he was serving became a casualty of enemy bombing. After good work he was the last to leave the ship with the Captain. Within minutes the ship blew up. Later in the war the young Griffithstown man was to be found in the Far East guarding Japanese prisoners. His brother Hubert served six years in the Royal Engineers and was at the Normandy landing before accompanying the allied forces to Germany.

After the war Jack, and his wife Betty, enjoyed a long and happy life

# STANLEY GROVE LLOYD
**Military Medal**

On the 21st July 1918, a son was born to Lillian Lloyd in Fowler Street, Wainfelin, Pontypool. He would grow up to be a hero.

With his sister, young Stan attended George Street School, Pontypool and left at an early age to work for Speed, the local baker. With the outbreak of war he joined the South Wales Borderers Regiment and served with them until 1946. On many occasions he did good work during ferocious fighting and was badly wounded when hit by shrapnel at the back of both legs and to the head. Allowing only the shortest of time for his wounds to heal he left hospital to return to his regiment who were engaged in heavy fighting. In December 1944, the *London Gazette* announced that the Military Medal had been awarded to Private Stanley Grove Lloyd, SWB, Pontypool. The account of the action for which he was commended states:

> 'On 11th September, 1944 during the entry into the outskirts of Le Havre, Private Lloyd was with the leading section of "B" Coy. When the tanks harboured in the road, the section was sent in front to search for enemy. It was dark when the section discovered a MG post near the cemetery. Private Lloyd took his bren gun and worked around the flank. Using his own initiative, he worked forward up to the enemy post, killed four of them and caused two to surrender.
>
> The next day he was again in the leading section advancing along a main road. Fire came from a side-street. Private Lloyd ran forward and lying in the open without cover fired continuously in the direction of the enemy, silencing their fire and preventing them from moving. Fifteen Germans surrendered in this position.
>
> Private Lloyd's boldness and disregard for his own safety on two occasions saved casualties in his section and enabled them to push quickly on.'

Abroad, and still involved in heavy fighting, the recently promoted Corporal Lloyd was unable to attend an award ceremony and his mother received the

Military Medal at her home in Fowler Street, Pontypool. Accompanying the medal was the following letter:

*Buckingham Palace*
*I regret that I am unable to give you personally the award, which you have so well earned.*
*I now send it to you with many congratulations and best wishes for your future happiness.*

*George RI.*
*3909874 Pte. S.G. Lloyd, M.M.*
*The South Wales Borderers*

Eva Watkins, an Oakdale girl supported the war effort by working at The Royal Ordnance Factory, Glascoed, and while walking through Pontypool with a girl friend a smart young man in uniform came into sight. Her friend introduced her to the polite soldier and it was the beginning of a long and loving relationship.

Stan Lloyd married Eva Watkins at the Cwrt a Bella Church, Oakdale, in 1947 and following his discharge from the army, he returned to work for Speed, the baker. Three children Christine, Ann and Kenneth were born following the happy event and Stan embarked on a plan that would give his young family a more secure future. He wisely became apprenticed as a carpenter and spent five years training at Oakdale Centre. With the qualification secured, he had regular employment for the remainder of his working life.

An enterprising gardener, neighbours often heared his melodious singing coming from the greenhouse at the top of his garden. A passionate follower of the game of rugby he was, for a time, a dedicated follower of Cwmbran R.F.C. He retained his military links by being a regular member of Pontnewynydd British Legion. This brave and likable man passed away at the Royal Gwent Hospital, Newport, on May 13, 1990.

# CYRIL JAMES McCANN
**Mentioned in Dispatches**

Cyril McCann had been a territorial from an early age and a keen member of the 2nd Monmouthshire Regiment's band. The son of Mr and Mrs Tom McCann, of Upper New Rank, Blaenavon, he followed the same occupation as his father. Work at the Blaenavon Company's Big Pit Colliery helped to keep him in peak physical condition and he would need all his strength to survive the difficult times ahead.

Married, with a young son named Malcolm, he had reached the ripe old age of thirty years when going on active service at the outbreak of war. In no time he reached the rank of Sergeant and took twenty-six stretcher-bearers to Normandy. Only six of these returned. The remainder were either killed, or taken prisoner. In December 1944, 4073524 Sgt. C.J. McCann received a well-earned Certificate of Merit signed by Field Marshall Montgomery. Later, in 1946, by the King's Order, the name of Sergeant C.J. McCann, South Wales Borderers, was published in the *London Gazette* for receiving a Mention in Dispatches for distinguished service.

Cyril returned to Blaenavon and attended many re-unions of his regiment. His interests included, specialising in rose growing, reading, writing, music, and being an accomplished cornet player. This likable man passed away in the year 2000.

# WILLIAM STANLEY MAGNESS
## Mentioned in Despatches

Born at School View, Pontymoile, Stan Magness would sadly have a short, but eventful life. His father, Mathew, was a steelworker and well-known Monmouthshire League referee, who officiated at many important games. Stan's early education took place at the Pontymoile Mixed Council School and within a short time of leaving he decided, in 1932, to join the Royal Navy. Before the war he served three years at a China station. He married a lass from Scotland, in 1939, and the issue of the happy marriage was a beautiful baby girl, which they named Margaret, after her mother. He would never see his daughter.

By 1941, Leading Seaman Magness had served on H.M.S. *Rodney*, Falmouth, the ill-fated *Royal Oak*, and in four submarines. In November 1941, he volunteered to be a member of a picked crew for the H.M.S. *Submarine Thorn*, which was about to go on special service in the Mediterranean.

On February 4th, 1942, Acting Petty Officer Magness displayed remarkable initiative and would later receive two awards for his courage. In May 1942, the Pontymoile man was Mentioned in Dispatches in the *London Gazette*, and the following year his wife took delivery of the Royal Humane Society's certificate on vellum, for life saving. His citation states:

> '*I am commanded by my Lord Commissioners of the Admiralty to send you the enclosed certificate of a Mention in Dispatches awarded by the King to your husband Acting Petty Officer William Stanley Magness, for his gallantry, skill, and devotion to duty while serving in H.M. Submarine Thorn in her first four Mediterranean war patrols. On one occasion PO Magness dived overboard in enemy waters to rescue a soldier who was drowning. Twice more he dived in to recover some loose gear; the loss of which might have hindered an important operation. Throughout these highly successful patrols this gallant Petty Officer's efficiency and good seamanship*

*were outstanding, and his coolness in heavy and prolonged depth charge counter-attacks was an inspiration to his shipmates. I am to express their Lordships' pleasure at this mark of His Majesty's high appreciation, and their deep regret that your husband did not live to receive it.*

*Your obedient servant,*
*H.M. Markam.'*

While on patrol in August of the same year the *Submarine Thorn* was spotted and sunk by Italian anti-submarine ships. All hands were lost.

Recently, Bill Moss, the young commando returning from a coastal raid and weighed down with equipment, and who would have drowned but for the prompt action of Petty Officer Magness, contacted Mrs Margaret Watkins, the hero's daughter. In a poignant letter he expressed his thanks for her father's courage all those years ago.

The name of D/JX 137447 Petty Officer William Stanley Magness can be seen on the Pontypool War Memorial and the Plymouth Naval War Memorial, Devon, which is situated centrally on The Hoe, looking directly towards Plymouth Sound.

# REGINALD IVOR MANNING
### Distinguished Flying Cross

Born June 15, 1918, Reg Manning would, in time, aspire to a splendid career in the Royal Air Force. As one of two sons born to Archie Manning, of Dowlais Street, Cwmbran, a collier at the local colliery, he attended St. Dial's School and later the West Monmouthshire School, Pontypool. While still at school the enterprising young Cwmbran lad held a temporary job as errand boy at the popular Rowland's Grocery Store, Cwmbran. Not long after leaving school he began a career with the Royal Air Force.

In 1935, and at the age of seventeen years, Reg Manning commenced three years apprentice training at RAF Halton and never looked back. A gradual rise in his chosen career would culminate with the former Cwmbran man becoming a Squadron Leader before he retired in 1964.

It is for his service during the Second World War that Squadron Leader Manning is still remembered by the Cwmbran inhabitants. As a young Flight Lieutenant, and a member of No. 76 Squadron, he took part in fifty dangerous operational flights in Halifax aircrafts over enemy occupied territory, and also took part in the bombing of the *Tirpitz*. In January 1945 he was awarded the Distinguished Flying Cross for: *'The utmost fortitude, courage and devotion to duty during operations against the enemy.'*

It would be an eventful year for Flight Lieutenant Manning. In April 1945, at Inkley Parish Church, West Yorkshire, he married Miss Margaret Mary Hirst, a pretty young WAAF. The long and happy marriage produced a son David Meredith and a daughter Susan Margaret.

Later in the year the modest Cwmbran hero received the Distinguished Flying Cross from King George VI at an investiture in the City Hall, Cardiff.

Reginald Ivor Manning remained in the Royal Air Force when the war finished and was granted a permanent commission as Engineering Officer. When he retired as a Squadron Leader in 1964, he at last found more time for his golf and bridge interests.

# ARNOLD STANLEY MEARA
## Distinguished Flying Cross

Born at Trevethin in 1914, the second of three
sons of Mr and Mrs R. Meara, builder and
contractor based in Abersychan. The family
lived at 'Brookville,' Cwmavon Road,
Abersychan. His education took place at
West Monmouthshire School, Pontypool, and
St. Catherine's College, Cambridge, where he
graduated in 1936. He was appointed science
master at Ruthin School, North Wales and in
1939 married Miss Mildred Williams,
youngest daughter of Alderman R.H.
Williams, a former Mayor of Ruthin.

A.S. Meara volunteered for the Royal Air
Force in October 1940 and received his
commissioned in April 1942. With 106 Squadron, he took part in all the 1,000
bomber raids on Germany and it was after his twenty-seventh operational flight
over enemy territory that the loss of his aircraft became known. After an anxious
wait his mother and wife were over-joyed to receive a letter in his own
handwriting from a German prison camp, which stated that he had fortunately
escaped from the aircraft and was well. Other members of his crew, however, had
not been so lucky.

In November 1942, it was announced that Pilot Officer Meara had been
awarded the Distinguished Flying Cross. The citation states:

> '*Pilot Officer Meara is a navigator of the highest skill, and throughout his
> operational sorties has maintained an exemplary standard of accuracy. He
> has navigated his aircraft to such targets as Bremen, Dusseldorf, Kassel,
> Nuremberg, and has been in all the more recent heavy raids on the Ruhr.
> By his efforts he has contributed largely to the success of two mining sorties.*'

When the war ended Pilot Officer A.S. Meara returned home safely from a
German prisoner-of-war camp and continued his teaching career.

# AUSTIN ARTHUR MEESE
## Military Medal

William Meese had worked for some time at the Cwmbran Brickworks as a firebrick maker, and while residing at 63 Belle Vue Road, it was but a short walk to his place of employment. He and his wife had four girls and two boys. It would be his youngest son Austin Arthur Meese, born April 5, 1909, who, through his brave deeds, will be remembered in perpetuity.

All the Meese children attended St. Dials School, Cwmbran. Austin left school at fifteen years of age and headed for London to make his fortune. His first job did not work out, but he soon settled into regular employment as a driver in the Midlands. In 1934 he married Doris Gertrude Massey in Dudley and two children, Shirley Maureen and Gavin, would be the result of the happy marriage.

In September 1939 he joined up and went to France almost immediately. He was at Dunkirk, and later left for India in April 1942. He would serve throughout the difficult Burma campaign.

During 1945, Lance Corporal Meese, of the Royal Army Service Corps, became involved in a number of daring actions, one of which earned him the award of the Military Medal. The account of the reported action for which he was commended states:

> '*On the night of the 24/25 February 1945, 5 Infantry Brigade commenced operations to force the crossing of the river Irrawaddy at Myittha and to secure the bridge head on the south bank of the river. It was initially planned that the crossing would be executed as a silent night operation, using infantry assault boats. However, as a result of early enemy interference with the crossing and difficulties encountered by the assault boats in the strong current, it became necessary to change this plan and to use Dukws for ferrying across the successive flights of assault infantry, although it was obvious that the size of the Dukws would present a good target to enemy fire. However, the Dukws carried out the task successfully, although not without*

*a considerable number of casualties to both crews and personnel being carried.*

*Lance Corporal Meese made six or seven crossings, and every time had to run the gauntlet of heavy enemy machine gun fire on both outward and return journeys. He showed outstanding courage and coolness and on reaching the north bank after each journey, was keen to pick up the next load and make another crossing with the least possible delay. The crossing was made particularly difficult by sandbanks and unknown currents, calling for great coolness in selecting the best channel. Lance Corporal Meese did not allow the enemy action to fluster him in these difficult circumstances when the slightest hesitation would have resulted in the Dukw going aground on the sandbanks. The topography of the channel required him to approach the south bank on which the enemy machine guns were sited almost head-on to within a short distance and then turn away broadside on.*

*I strongly recommend Lance Corporal Meese for the award.'*

Due to the on-going war, the medal was presented to T/50059 Lance Corporal A.A. Meese by the Army Commander, with a letter of congratulations from H.R.H. King George VI.

Austin transferred to the Army Reserve in 1946 and returned to Britain to live with his wife and two children at Tudor Street, Tipton, Staffs. He continued his employment as a lorry driver for many years. A keen sports fan he regularly attended football and cricket matches. In 1987, this brave man passed away in Dudley.

# JOHN WALTER MOORE
### Distinguished Flying Cross

Born 1923, the only son of Mr and Mrs Walter Moore, Clarence Street, Pontypool. His parents managed their butchers shop in Clarence Street while John attended the nearby Park Terrace and West Monmouthshire Schools. Before he was nineteen years of age he volunteered to defend his country and was allowed to join up in 1941.

The young Pontypool man took part in numerous operational flights over occupied territory for which he was awarded the Distinguished Flying Cross. He also received a silver cup from the 'skipper' of his bomber, who presented one to each of the crew as a token of appreciation.

Throughout the war Pilot Officer Moore travelled all over the world by air until arriving safely home at the end of hostilities.

# ADONIS MORGAN
## Military Medal

Born August 18, 1913, in Blaenavon, the son of
Charles Morgan, of The Oaks, a miner then
steelworker. Adonis Morgan was one of four
boys and one girl. Early education took place at
the old Park Street School, Blaenavon.

Before the war Adonis, or Terry, an alias,
which he preferred to use, was a well-known
amateur boxer regularly training and taking part
in bouts in the boxing rooms behind the old
Forge Hammer Public House. As a member of
the 2nd Battalion, Royal Welch Fusiliers, he
took part in the fierce fighting on the Burma
front between March 1942 and 1945. The
Regiment endured many months of difficult
campaigning in thick, hot jungle, while soaked
to the skin for days in torrential monsoon rain.
In 1944, and at about four in the morning, just
as the moon was going down, Fusilier Morgan
saw some forty men approaching his position. He shouted, "Halt!" and was
answered by a grenade, which hit his gun muzzle and bounced out of the gun pit.
The explosion badly injured his right hand, left shoulder and the side of his face.
What followed would earn the thirty-year-old Blaenavon man the immediate
award of the Military Medal. The official citation states:

'On the night of 5/6 March 1944, a Carrier Platoon locality was attacked
by a party of 30 to 40 Japanese. Fusilier Morgan was acting as No 1 on a
Bren gun. He opened fire and a hand grenade burst within a few feet of
him. Morgan was wounded in his left arm and chest, and his No 2 was hit
in the arm and head. The Section Commander brought No 2 to Platoon
HQ, and on his return to the section post found Fusilier Morgan attempting
to remove the empty magazine from his gun and place a fresh one on with
his wounded left hand. Grenades were still bursting in the vicinity. The
section commander assisted him to do this and Morgan continued firing,
inflicting further casualties on the Japanese until ordered out by his Section
Commander to receive attention.

Fusilier Morgan showed great coolness and steadiness in this action. His
soldierly conduct in continuing to fire, although severely wounded and in

*great pain, effectively broke up the Japanese attack and deserves the highest praise.'*

Fusilier Morgan's wounds soon healed with the correct medical attention, but he would always have problems with his injured left hand and never boxed again. His interest in boxing never waned and he always kept to a training regime while promoting local bouts.

Terry married Christina (Betty) Maunders of Blaenavon, at Llanwenarth Chapel, Govilon, on St. David's Day, 1959. He would have no children of his own, but inherited several delightful stepchildren and grandchildren. He was employed for the remainder of his working life in Panteg Steelworks. Although a non-drinker, or smoker, this popular man was well known as an excellent crib player and responsibly organised many military concerts in the Workmens Hall, Blaenavon. Until his health failed him he never missed his Regiment's re-unions and always attended the Blaenavon Armistice Day service. This proud, valley gentleman passed away on June 26, 1996, age 83 years.

# GARFIELD MORGAN
### Mentioned in Dispatches

An old boy of the local school he became well known, respected, and remembered by many with great affection. Garfield Morgan, the son of Mr and Mrs J.H. Morgan, Station Road, Pontnewydd, left school at fourteen years of age and went to work for his uncle, Bert Poulton, a well-established Pontnewydd butcher. Quite content with his lot at the time, he enjoyed a healthy interest in sport. He became a useful amateur boxer, and for those days, had a prestigious trial for Newport A.F.C. During these blissful years Garfield married and his wife, Elsie, gave birth to two children, Michael and Margaret.

Residing at Upper Cwmbran it was but a short journey to his place of employment and there was an order about his young life. Unfortunately, this would soon be disrupted with the outbreak of war. Feeling the need to do 'his bit,' the twenty-eight year old joined the Army in May 1940.

Sergeant Garfield Morgan, Royal Artillery, landed at Sword Beach on D-Day and proceeded to the famous Pegasus Bridge. Here his battery set up their guns and went into action. In his diary Sergeant Morgan wrote:

'D-Day June 6th 1944.
> Landed on D-Day June 6th with second wave at 2 o'clock. Met Lt. Bird at beachhead. Took coast road down to Hermanville. Set up gun site on road, large cornfield on right, fenced in, and with notices of 'Auctian Mines.' Why should a cornfield be mined?
> Saw a lot of action on this site. One early morning raid, Jerry dropped a load of incendiary bombs from overhead, three, which dropped in the gun pit. I quickly disposed of these with sandbags; this was no act of bravery, but one of self-preservation. I was London Gazetted and Mentioned in Dispatches, which entitles me to wear Oak Leaves on my medal ribbons. We saw quite a bit of action on this site, dawn and evening raids...'

Around this time Sergeant Morgan came across a shell signed by Miss Grace Williams, a war worker, of Queen Street, Pontypool. The battery commander immediately forwarded a letter of thanks and good wishes to her.

With the war over Garfield returned to work in his uncle's shop. When his uncle retired, he took over the business. He attended many meetings of his old regiment in Newport and was a member of the Normandy Veteran's Association, Cardiff. This brave and popular man died peacefully at the Royal Gwent Hospital, Newport, on 26th October 2001, age 89 years.

# VIOLET MAY MORGAN
### Mentioned in Dispatches

Violet Morgan's father was born in Mamhilad in 1865 and his genial disposition made him exceedingly popular with all sections of the community. John Morgan entered the service of the Great Western Railway Company as a ticket collector at the age of eighteen years and as the years passed he reached the important post of Chief Divisional Inspector. For twenty years he was chairman of Panteg Horticultural Society and gave tremendous support to St. Mary's Church, Panteg. He and his wife Catherine lived at 'Sunleigh' Pontypool Road, Panteg, and just prior to his death he was elected to the responsible post of chairman of Panteg Council. Of Mr Morgan it might truly be said that he was loved by everyone who knew him, for he had realised the vital truth that 'We pass this way but once' and had worked untiringly to leave the world a better place than he found it. Without any doubt it is certain that he passed his commendable qualities to his children. Sadly, he died in 1932 and would not know about his youngest child's remarkable act of heroism.

Born May 7, 1902, at Pontypool, Violet and her brother and two sisters all attended the local schools. At an early age she made up her mind to lead a life of compassion and on completion of her education took up nurse training at Bristol Royal Infirmary. She qualified as a nurse and later returned to her studies to pass further examinations to qualify and practise in the highly responsible position of a District Nurse. Her brother John H. Morgan became an outfitter in Griffithstown, sister Lillian married Mr Mansell Morgan, headmaster of Pontymoel Schools, and her other sister, Gladys, married Mr Harry Dowding, of Weymouth. After her father's death in 1932, Violet and her mother moved to Weymouth, where she was allocated a house for the use of District Nursing staff. To carry out her work she cycled everywhere for many years until allowed to have a small car. Her beloved car, which she named 'Tilley,' served her well throughout her remaining working years. By 1940, Violet had been employed in Weymouth as a Queen's Nurse for seven years with the Westham District Nursing Association. On August 11 of that year she showed tremendous courage during a heavy enemy air attack on the coastal town of Weymouth. With bombs dropping all around she observed an injured and helpless ambulance driver in an exposed position near her first aid post. Immediately she threw herself across the prostrate lady, a Miss Harding, and prevented her from further injury. As bombs continued to rain down, Nurse Morgan further distinguished herself by dressing injuries received by the depot personnel. For her courage Violet Morgan was Mentioned in Dispatches in the *London Gazette*. The letter received by Nurse Morgan from the Ministry of Home security is as follows:

'I am directed by the Minister of Home Security to inform you that Sir Geoffrey Peto, Regional Commissioner for the South-West Region, drew his attention to the courage and presence of mind which you displayed during an enemy attack on August last. The Ministry have greatly appreciated your praiseworthy conduct on this occasion and the matter was brought to the notice of his Majesty the King, who was graciously pleased to give orders for the publication of your name as having received an expression of commendation for your services.'

For her heroism, in November of the same year, Lady Ilchester on behalf of the Dorset County Nursing Association also presented Nurse Morgan with an inscribed chiming clock.

Violet never married. Much loved by her patients, medical colleagues and family, she led a full life indulging in foreign travel and a love of music. Her skill playing the organ at the local church was very much appreciated by the parishioners. Walking in the country became a great pleasure and often she would jump into her small, well-serviced car and explore the highways and byways.

This gentle lady with a pleasing personality, who had inherited many of her father's good qualities, died in 1990, at Weymouth.

# MANSEL HERBERT MURGATROYD
## Military Medal

Born April 13, 1924, the son of Harry and Winifred May Murgatroyd, 6, Prince Street, Pontypool. Harry Murgatroyd was a native of Yorkshire and served in the King's Own Yorkshire Light Infantry during the 1st World War. Badly wounded, he received treatment at Panteg Hospital, Griffithstown, a temporary military hospital. It was during his convalescence he met Winifred Pearce, the daughter of a Pontypool businessman. They fell in love and Harry settled in the Eastern Valley. Harry took up employment as a 'roller' at Pontnewynydd Ironworks and in his leisure time enjoyed the game of rugby. Up to 1927, he had played seven seasons for Pontypool and a number of Rugby League games under an alias. Three fine children would be the issue of the happy marriage, Mansel, Walter and Irene. With his brother and sister, Mansel's education  took place at George Street School. In his spare time he worked as a butcher's boy for Porters, of the market, Pontypool. The remainder of his free time was taken up as a member of the Boys' Brigade and playing football, his favourite team at the time being Lovell's United, Newport. With his education completed he worked for a time at Roly Morgan's Emporium, Pontypool, and later at Pilkington Brothers' Glass Works. On 5 November 1942, he was called up for military service and entered the South Wales Borderers Regiment.

In June 1944, Private Murgatroyd took an active part in a battle, which ranks in the long and treasured history of the South Wales Borderers as one of their finest hours. The well known Chateau de Sully, found on the French coast, was one of the chief objectives of the Borderers following a rough landing during which they experienced some stiff fighting. They fought the Huns to a standstill, and then came the critical stage before the advance inland could be continued. It was imperative to link up with the Americans. Before that could be done a river bridgehead had to be forced and the Chateau at Sully captured.

The river was crossed successfully, but the Chateau stood firm like an impregnable fortress, for the Germans obviously realised its critical importance as one of the strong points of their coastal defence. It was honeycombed with concrete works, steel machine gun posts and deep underground shelters. Well-concealed field works surrounded the whole of this formidable structure set in difficult countryside. But it had to be taken and it was taken on the morning of June 8, the morning when the order was given to attack.

Every man in the South Wales Borderers knew what he was up against and none hesitated. The first attack was beaten back, but they were not to be denied. Again and again they stormed at the Chateau. It was a grim battle for every man from the commanding officer, who was seriously wounded, to the cooks and orderlies. They all fought the Germans to the bitter end.

The Chateau was captured and all objectives seized. The South Wales Borderers had saved the day with many acts of bravery. One courageous act witnessed Private Mansel Murgatroyd continuing to give protective fire with his Bren gun until he dropped from the loss of blood. He returned to a hospital in the Midlands for medical treatment.

Alert to the entries of gallantry awards in the *London Gazette*, friends of Harry Murgatroyd were quick to suggest he looked in the 31 August 1944, edition. He was pleased to read that No. 14327980 Private Mansel Herbert Murgatroyd, South Wales Borderers, Pontypool, had been awarded the Military Medal. The full citation states:

> 'On 8th June , 1944, during an attack on Sully, Private Murgatroyd, who was in charge of a Bren gun, whilst under heavy machine gun fire moved his gun forward and gave protection to his section to enable them to continue their advance.
>
> Although badly wounded he continued to operate his gun until no longer able to do so. He displayed courage of a very high order and by his action undoubtedly saved many lives.'

Fully recovered from the serious wounds and home on leave, Private Murgatroyd attended a special presentation evening at the Pontypool Comrades Club. As a son of a long serving member, Private Murgatroyd, MM., was handed a gift by Mr. J.H. Thompson, President of the Club. During leave Mansel met a young land army girl based at Builth Wells and they fell in love. Soon they became engaged. Peggy and her future mother-in-law became great friends, as witnessed by the many delightful letters received at Prince Street, Pontypool.

Rejoining his Regiment there would be no respite from the ferocious fighting. On Monday, 22 January 1945, Private Mansel H. Murgatroyd, MM., was sadly killed in action and lies in the Jonkerbosch War Cemetery, Netherlands.

# WILLIAM JAMES NIBLETT
**Military Medal**

Born June 22, 1919, at Pontnewydd, Monmouthshire. His father, Edward Niblett, was at the time employed at Tynewydd Works, Pontnewydd, and later he became the landlord of a public house in Bridge Street, Griffithstown. Jim Niblett attended the church school in Pontnewydd with his two brothers and three sisters before taking up employment at Panteg Steelworks. Until the outbreak of war the young man had made his home with his youngest sister Mrs E. Phillips, of Hawthorn Road, Sebastopol, Torfaen. In January 1940, Jim Niblett joined the 2nd Monmouthshire Regiment and went to war.

In Kent, Jim met an attractive young lady serving with the ATS and attached to his Regiment. A romance blossomed and he married Mary Grady, from Widnes, at the Pontypool Registry Office in 1943. Both had leave due to them, but the army allowed three extra days, which made a full week for the young couple to celebrate the happy event. Mary remained in the ATS until her first child was born. They would have three children, Maureen, Edward and Lyndon.

With his regiment he landed in north-west Europe eight days after D-Day and as they fought their way towards Germany he experienced a great deal of ferocious fighting. Promotion came quickly and in September and November 1944, he earned two Certificates of Merit. Further bravery on October 22, 1944, gave the twenty five year old a well-deserved Military Medal. The official history of the regiment states:

> '...5th Division, concentrating to the westward, was preparing to attack Hertogenbosch, a large town that had been bypassed in the thrust towards Arnhem...Sgt. W.J. Niblett's platoon of "C" Company soon after crossing

*the start line had to pass over an exposed piece of ground and came under heavy and accurate fire from at least two spandau posts which were well dug in. Sgt. Niblett ordered his platoon to lie down and give covering fire, while he, seizing a Bren from the nearest section, dashed forward alone and in full view of the enemy, firing his Bren from the hip. Going straight for one of the posts, he reached it safely, and emptied his magazine at the occupants, killing all three of them. His quick grasp of the situation and his immediate action had direct results on the operation for they enabled the speed of the advance to be maintained at a time when a check may have proved fatal to success. Throughout this day and the next Sgt. Niblett commanded his platoon with skill and daring and wherever the fighting was thickest, he was to be found cheering on his men. The Military Medal, which was awarded to him, was thoroughly well earned.'*

In September 1945 Field Marshal Montgomery pinned the ribbon of the Military Medal on the chest of Sergeant Niblett at an Investiture in Dusseldorf and for five days in October he was the guest of the inhabitants of Hertogenbosch, Holland. Later he attended Buckingham Palace with his sister to have the Military Medal presented to him by King George VI.

Jim returned home and lived for many years in Cwmbran. He worked as an office manager for the construction firm McAlpine and continued in the Territorial Army for a number of years. He became a keen member of Cwmbran British Legion and took a great interest in the local sporting scene. Eventually the McAlpine company weren't doing so well in the Cwmbran area and Jim had to be based in Cardiff.

This man of tremendous courage died on October 28, 2001, in a nursing home in Splot, Cardiff. He would have a large military funeral in Cwmbran.

# PERCY FORDE PAYNE
**Military Cross**

Major the Reverend Percy Forde Payne was the only son of Mr and Mrs H. Payne, formerly of 'Warminster,' Mount Pleasant, Pontnewynydd. An old boy of Abersychan Secondary School, his first job was working in the offices of Messrs Partridge Jones and John Paton Ltd. He was inducted to the pastorate of Stow Park Presbyterian Church, Newport, in September 1936, and resigned that pastorate in 1941, when it was obvious that there would not be an early ending to the war.

In 1938 he married Miss Olwen Thomas, a teacher at Cwmffrwdoer School, and the daughter of Mr and Mrs Charles Thomas, Hanbury Road, Pontnewynydd, Monmouthshire.

Having volunteered to become a Chaplain to the Forces when an appeal was made to young ministers, he was called up in October, 1939. He served with the Welsh Guards in France until May 1940, when he was evacuated with his unit from Boulogne. He spent the next four years in various parts of Britain and again landed in France just after D-Day.

While still serving with the Welsh Guards in 1945, he would always be in the thick of the action while the famous regiment led in the race across France. He wrote: *'I well remember on one occasion during a particularly hot period, when we were getting more than our fair share of mortaring and when the rain was pouring down on us...Guardsman Holvey, from Blaenavon, and we both thought how nice it would be to visit the Workmen's Hall or the Pavilion. Then a shower of German mortars came down and drove such pleasures from our minds...I served with the Guards Armoured Division from its formation, and remained with them all through the Normandy battles, where our casualties were heavy. It fell to my sad lot to bury many of the men from the Eastern Valley who were killed, and that they were from my own area made it a heartbreaking task. I could see only too clearly the streets from which they came.'*

It was in August 1944, while the padre was returning to a battered aid post during the battle of Le Pas Perrier, that he distinguished himself and earned the esteem of the whole regiment. For his bravery that day he was awarded the

Military Cross.  The official citation states:

> 'With only one man to help him, Captain Payne, who was exposed for a whole day to concentrated shellfire, evacuated nearly a hundred casualties from a battered aid post during the battle of Le Pas Perrier last August.
>
> He had just returned from visiting a forward company when the Regimental Aid Post was hit by shells, which killed seven wounded men and knocked out all the Medical Officer's staff save one.
>
> The Padre, although himself slightly wounded, immediately took complete charge, organised every passing vehicle into an ambulance, and managed to clear the Regimental Aid Post of the dead and wounded and get it into action again.
>
> After being relieved, though almost exhausted, he began his task of seeing that each man killed had a proper and reverent burial.'

Reverend Payne was extremely sad to transfer from the Welsh Guards.  He would write:

> 'Just as we were being relieved I received my promotion, and it meant, unfortunately, that I had to leave the Welsh Guards.  It was a very great blow to me; I had been so long with them and knew them so intimately.  They fought magnificently and no Padre has been privileged to serve a finer regiment.  They have won fresh laurels for themselves, and brought great honour to Wales and Monmouthshire.'

For perpetuity the esteem for which the Pontnewynydd padre was held is recorded in the regiment's history:

> 'It was the last of such services conducted by the Reverend P.F. Payne, C.F., who was leaving the 1st Battalion on promotion.  He had served with the Regiment almost throughout the war, having been with the 2nd Battalion at Boulogne in 1940 and with the 1st Battalion throughout their fighting in Normandy, Belgium and Holland.  The War Diary did not overstate the facts when it put on record, "He will be missed by every officer and man in the Battalion."  A true Welshman, he was loved and respected by all ranks and his forthcoming departure seems seemed to them to involve "a disastrous change."'

# WILLIAM REES POOLEY
### Military Medal

Born William Rees Pooley, on December 15, 1913, near Aberdare. His father James Pooley had always been a collier and came over to the Pontypool district from Aberaman in search of regular work. He, and his wife and their four boys and three girls settled at Victoria Village. With his brothers and sisters young Bill attended Victoria Village School until leaving age when he commenced work on a lorry delivering coal.

When seventeen years of age Bill joined the King's Shropshire Light Infantry and became an army-boxing champion. Stationed at the outbreak of war in Alton, he married Margaret (Peg) Jones, a young lady from the small town. A daughter Jennifer was the issue of this long and happy marriage.

During June 1944, in recognition of gallant and distinguished service in Italy, the King approved the award of the Military Medal to Corporal (Acting Sergeant) William Rees Pooley, Kings Shropshire Light Infantry, of Pontypool. Bill later wrote an account of action, which earned the Military Medal:

> 'APRIL 15 1944.
> We were 3-4 miles north of Anzio when we came under heavy shelling. My Platoon Commander (Lieutenant Vines) with a runner went forward to check the position of the enemy. A short while later the runner returned saying the Platoon Commander had been wounded. I asked if he was still alive, but the runner did not know. I said, "I've got to find him," so I crawled 100-120 yards and found him badly wounded in the back, but still alive.
>
> I then got him on my back and crawled to our line, which was still under heavy shelling, but I will never forget the look in his eyes as he said, "I knew you would come Corporal." Alas, he died three weeks later. What a brave man and only twenty-three years of age.'

After the war Bill Pooley became an outdoor construction worker and one of his first jobs was helping to build the large British Nylon Spinners Factory, near Pontypool. For the remainder of his working life he enjoyed working for the well-known McAlpine construction company. His leisure time was filled as a member of the Conservative Club, Pontypool, gardening, and as a keen supporter of sport, particularly boxing.

This cheerful, brave and caring man died in September 1998 and was buried at Panteg Cemetery, Torfaen.

# KENNETH ARTHUR PRITCHARD
## Mentioned in Dispatches

Born October 23, 1916 at 'Hawthorns' Waterloo, Talywain, Monmouthshire. His father, George Arthur Pritchard, came from the nearby district of Garndiffaith and was employed for the most part of his working life as a chauffer. While living at 'Homelea,' Manor Road, Abersychan, Ken attended the British School and Abersychan Technical School until becoming a clerk at Crumlin Valley Colliery.

Fully aware of how serious the war with Germany had become Ken Pritchard joined the Royal Air Force in 1940. Almost immediately he was sent overseas. Later he did good work during the evacuation of the British forces from Greece and was one of the last to leave just before the enemy arrived. For this valuable work Aircraftsman (First Class) Arthur Kenneth Pritchard was Mentioned in Dispatches and awarded the Oak Leaf to wear on his campaign medal ribbon. His hand written account of the perilous time states:

> 'Duke Ellison and I had been at Argos for a day, after a three day trip by road, down from Athens. We were at a school, about a mile from the docks; waiting with a few hundred others for nightfall – seven or eight hours away – when we were due to proceed to board a few small ships waiting for us.
>
> Volunteers were called for, (You and You) for a job on a drome a couple of miles away, for a matter of a few hours. Thinking it would help time to pass more quickly, we didn't try to wangle out of it and in a few minutes we were on our way by lorry. We were to stop all traffic and ascertain its destination, then, if we were satisfied, allow it to proceed.
>
> We arrived at the drome about three o'clock – a lovely sunny afternoon it was too. We had a look around, noticed the Blenheims and Lysanders standing forlornly on the drome and took up our position, just at its side, at the road junction. Our armament for this job was terrific! – two rifles, 50

rounds each – two service revolvers, 12 rounds each – and our own revolvers, each with at least 100 rounds.

We sat for about an hour on some unused 500 lbs bombs, yarning and discussing our chances of getting out of Greece. We saw a shower of Jerry kites going over, at about 3,000 feet, and these, without any trouble at all, proceeded to bomb the dock area. This didn't make us feel any happier because our boats were there.

The raid lasted about twenty minutes, then Jerry went serenely back – no trouble at all. The sky over the docks was thick with smoke. (Glad we were in the quiet).

Almost immediately we saw our five Hurricanes taking off from their small drome, a mile or so away, and flying out to sea. They looked lovely!

Immediately afterwards, we saw some more kites, coming in over the hills to the North, not very high. We knew they must be Jerry, because we didn't have that many! Those poor devils at the docks are due to get some more, we thought, but we soon altered our minds when they started circling the drome. We nipped smartly for the only cover available – the yard high corn in the field at the side of the drome. Jerry had not the slightest opposition, each machine did a couple of dummy runs and then, in line astern came in, dropping incendiaries and small explosives – 50 pounders we thought.

In a very short time we were cheesed off doing nothing, so we decided to "have a go" with our rifles. The kites were doing a shallow dive over the drome, turning to climb away for another circuit just over our heads. We estimated their speed at about 80 m.p.h. and decided to have a try just when they were starting their climbing turn, showing us all their lower surface. They were ME 109s and Dorniers - the latter we considered our meat. In a matter of minutes our ammo was gone, so we decided to make a run for it, to reach an old Lewis Machine Gun standing about 200 yards away. Maybe we could get it going and bag ourselves a couple of Jerries – we must have been mad! Still, it didn't seem quite right to be doing nothing when our kites were being destroyed before our eyes.

We reached the gun o.k., and there was a pan of ammunition in place. Duke fired a couple of bursts, then I had a go – in a matter of seconds this ammo had gone. No good had been done as far as we could see; all that we had done was to attract our visitors' attention. A few 109s came along to attend to us – and we, having no ammo, could only get away from the now useless gun and lie in the grass praying. I was scared! A horrible feeling deep inside me. On this warm day, covered in sweat, I was cold, shivering. All my past life was going before me, like pictures on a movie screen – home was so dear to me then. Duke and I, lying side by side in the grass, shook hands. They machine-gunned the ground around the gun, bullets were singing in the grass, then suddenly all was silent, our visitors had gone.

Duke and I got to our feet, I remember how we each gave a weak laugh. The kites on the drome were ablaze, ammo popping around from their guns, but the roar of engines had gone. The air was thick with smoke of incendiaries and burning aircraft. We were alive without a single scratch.

We returned to our post at the road junction at the corner of the drome, and almost immediately a staff car came tearing up with Air Commodore Gregson. He was very nice, asked us if we had enjoyed the raid and wanted to know if the defence guns had been in action. It appears that there were four Bofors and four Lewis guns and their crews. We told him our information and that we hadn't heard or seen anyone else. Suddenly the air seemed full of kites – the three of us threw ourselves to the deck, only to rise again almost immediately and laughing. Our Hurricanes had returned with their "charges" – ten Lockheed Transports. He was amazed at our story, congratulated us, and said, "You'll be hearing more about this." H e then asked if we were prepared to carry on duty until nightfall, if he could provide more ammunition and food. As we agreed he left us for nearly half an hour, but returned with a couple of hundred rounds for the rifles and food – biscuits and bully beef with a bottle of beer. A lovely feast it was too, with the smoke slowly clearing from the drome and the sun sinking to the west in a beautiful blaze of glory.

We never knew for certain if our action had been in any way successful – all we knew was that two of the Dorniers had force landed just a few miles away, and no one else had been firing at them.'

Later, Ken Pritchard went for pilot training and received his wings. He completed the war as a flight sergeant.

With the terrible war over, Ken met a pretty WAAF while stationed in Southport. He married Peggy May Lilley, of Southport, during the Christmas period of 1946, and later a son, Ian, was born.

The young married couple returned to live at 'Homelea,' Abersychan and Ken continued his employment as a clerk at Crumlin Valley Colliery. He had various office management positions throughout the remainder of his working life. For a long period of time he supported the Noddfa Baptist Church and became the secretary of its Sunday School.

This brave man died in 1965 age 48 years.

# WILLIAM JOHN RALPH
## Distinguished Flying Cross

Born in Abertillery in 1915. He was the son of Margaret and S. Abner Ralph, 4, Clarence Place, Pontypool. Abner Ralph, a director of the well-known Ralph's Omnibus Company, based in Abertillery, came to live in Pontypool with the intention of setting up another garage and service centre in the town, but after a short time the firms main interests returned to the Western Valley. Abner immediately took a great liking to Pontypool and settled in the town. He was to take an active role in many of the town's activities. In 1950, Ralph's Buses were taken over by the British Transport Commission and Abner retired eighteen months later. His only son Jack attended West Monmouthshire School and Cardiff Technical College.

Before enlisting Jack had been an engineer in Cardiff, but the call to duty became too strong and he joined the Royal Air Force Volunteer Reserve in 1941. With aircrew training completed in Canada and America, he was commissioned in 1943.

In August 1944, King George VI was pleased to approve the award of the Distinguished Flying Cross in recognition of many successful operations against the enemy, during which high skill, fortitude and devotion to duty were displayed by Acting Flight Lieutenant Ralph, 156709, RAFVR, No. 90 Squadron.

After thirty flights over enemy occupied territory he was grounded for a time and given instructional duties. This brave young man survived the war and a happy marriage produced four children: David, Anne, John and Bridget. Jack and his family settled in Bournemouth where he became managing director of Shamrock and Rambler Coaches Ltd and Charlie's Car's Ltd.

# SIDNEY DANIEL JORDAN-REARDON
## Brigade Gallantry Certificate

Born on April 4, 1920, the third son of Mr and Mrs Daniel Reardon, 32 The Avenue, Wainfelin, Pontypool, Sidney Reardon was a true son of Pontypool. His father ran a successful bakery and confectionary business in Wainfelin Avenue. Young Sid attended St. Alban's and Twmpath School, before transferring to the senior Abersychan Technical School.

Leaving school at fifteen years of age, he sought employment with the Gas and Water Company at Abersychan. Prior to the outbreak of war he joined the Panteg Battery, Royal Artillery, based at Griffithstown, and was mobilised with them immediately hostilities began.

As a soldier in the Royal Artillery, he soon became the youngest Sergeant in the Regiment and served with them all through the war. While on leave a pretty young lady, who was the daughter of a Pontypool butcher, caught his eye. He married Constance Mary Porter in St. Alban's Roman Catholic Church, Pontypool, in 1943, and Phillipa Catherine Ann, a beautiful baby girl was born.

Always a solid non-commissioned officer Sidney Reardon did particularly good work in 1944. This is witnessed in a certificate signed by the Brigadier of the South Wales Infantry Brigade:

> 'Rank: Bdr. Name: Reardon. S. Regt. 133 Field Regiment R.A.
> *I congratulate you on your outstanding service and devotion to duty during the campaign from 22 June to 31 December 1944.'*

After World War Two, work at British Nylon Spinners, near Pontypool, became his main occupation for forty years. He had played rugby in his regiment and remained a keen supporter of the game for the remainder of his life. Known to be a good horseman in his younger days, later life was spent playing golf and attending meetings of Pontypool Probus Club. He passed away on May 17, 1996.

# GWYN LLOYD ROBERTS
## Distinguished Flying Cross

Born in 1922, the only son of Mr and Mrs J. Stanley Roberts, 16 Dingle Road, Pontypool. His parents regularly attended St. David's Hall Presbyterian Church, Pontypool and Gwyn, and his twin sisters, Joan and Peg, received their early schooling at Twmpath Central School. Mr Roberts, senior, worked in the office of Crumlin Valley Colliery and at the outbreak of war was Lieutenant Quartermaster of Pontypool Company, of the 9th Battalion Monmouthshire Home Guard.

Gwyn left school in 1937, at the age of fifteen years, and immediately enlisted in the Royal Air Force. He enjoyed his early days and later played a regular game of rugby for his squadron. He did his first operational flight on his 21st birthday. By 1944 he had become a flight engineer and as a member of a Pathfinder Squadron, had taken part in fifty operational flights over enemy territory before being grounded. In 1944, the Pontypool man was deservedly awarded the Distinguished Flying Cross for gallantry in the air. The citation reads:

> '*In his capacity of Flight-Engineer this Warrant Officer has always displayed outstanding efficiency and his keenness to operate has been commendable at all times. Recently, during an attack on Berlin, while on the bombing run, his aircraft was heavily engaged by ground defences and was severely damaged, one engine catching fire. By his prompt action Warrant Officer Roberts prevented the flames from spreading and enabled his captain to complete his attack successfully. On all sorties when over heavily defended targets in emergencies he has performed his duties with coolness and skill.*'

Warrant Officer Gwyn Lloyd Roberts, DFC, survived the terrible war and lived for many years in Huntingdon, Cambridge. He passed away on September 21, 1976.

# MOSTYN LLEWELLYN ROWLAND
## Distinguished Flying Medal

Mostyn Rowland belongs to an old and respected Cwmbran family. His great-grandfather, Sidney Rowland, had for some time carried on in business at Abbey Road as a grocer and corn merchant. In 1885 he linked up the grocery section of the business with that of a bakery and confectioners. Later, in need of larger premises, Mostyn's father purchased a site in Ventnor Road, Cwmbran. Just prior to the outbreak of war, and in order to pursue other interests, he began to place the thriving business into the hands of his two sons. The war would change everything. Mostyn joined the Royal Air Force Volunteer Reserve in 1941; his elder brother Leslie, enlisted in 1939 and crossed over to France. His job was troop carrying attached to the Royal Army Service Corps. Fortunately, he returned safely from the Dunkirk set-back.

Flight Sergeant Rowland had passed out as an observer by 1942, and then went through the usual anti-submarine patrol work before taking part in raids over Germany and the occupied countries. He did twenty-eight operational flights to Berlin, Essen, Dortmund, Pilsen, Spezzia, Hamburg and other places. On one occasion he had to bale out, but sustained only a damaged ankle. On another return journey his craft came down off the west coast of Scotland, and the crew had to take to their dingy. They were rescued after a few hours.

In October 1944, the name of Sergeant Rowland appeared in the *London Gazette*. He had deservedly been awarded the Distinguished Flying Medal and his citation states:

> *'This airman has invariably set his mind on the task in hand fearlessly and with a fine fighting spirit. His skill and cool determination when over the target area has ensured the success of a number of missions. During his first tour of operation with his squadron, Flight Sergeant Rowland has displayed great ability and courage as a bomb aimer.'*

A few weeks later Sergeant Rowland received a letter of sincere congratulations from the Urban District Council of Cwmbran at his home in Coronation Road. 1944 had proved to be an important year for Mostyn. On June 26th, he had special leave to marry Margaret Miles, of Pontnewydd. The wedding took place at the Holy Trinity Church, Pontnewydd, and a daughter Adele would be the issue of the happy union.

After the war Mostyn returned to the family business and became a founder member of the Cwmbran Chamber of Trade. A further interest in local politics resulted in election as a councillor for the Llantarnam district. Eventual retirement to Bournemouth gave him the opportunity to become chairman for nine years of the local Air Crew Association, a voluntary post that he thoroughly enjoyed. Mostyn is still playing a good game of bowls and keeps in regular contact with his daughter Adele, who lives in Canada.

# DENNIS WILLIAM SEABOURNE
## Mentioned in Despatches

Born July 26, 1907, at Railway Terrace, Sebastopol, near Pontypool. At the age of four years, Dennis Seabourne went to live in the nearby village of New Inn and attended the local school. At thirteen years of age he assisted as a pupil teacher until the time he left school. At fourteen years, he worked down the pit for a week until his parents found out and wouldn't let him continue. Two years later he went to the Brecon Depot of the South Wales Borderers Regiment and told the recruiting sergeant that he was seventeen years of age. His parents were in hot pursuit and told the military authorities his correct age. A year later, and without informing his parents, he took the King's shilling and signed on for twelve years. The twelve years was spent in India and China with the South Wales Borderers Regiment.

Unemployed and twenty-nine years of age, he met Eleanor May Jones in Pontypool. She was the daughter of Mr. William Jones, a master cabinetmaker residing in Picton Street, Griffithstown. After a short courtship they married at St. Hilda's Church, Griffithstown, on September 21, 1936. The long and happy marriage produced a son Gordon and daughters June and Sandra. It would not be long before Dennis found secure employment as a ironworker.

In 1941, and thirty-four years of age, Dennis Seabourne put his long military experience to good use by joining the Home Guard. He soon became a Sergeant and it wasn't on a foreign battlefield that the local man showed great bravery, but near his home. For the courageous act he would be 'Mentioned in Despatches' in the *London Gazette* and have the right to wear an Oak Leaf on his medal ribbon.

According to the citation in the *London Gazette*, Sergeant Seabourne, an instructor attached to the Headquarters of the Pontypool Home Guard, was instructing a party of Home Guards in grenade throwing on a Sunday in February 1944. Unfortunately, a grenade thrown by a Private struck the parapet in front of the throwing bay and rolled back towards the two men. The Private moved towards the live grenade, but Sergeant Seabourne realising the immediate danger, pulled him away and placed his body between the recruit and the bomb to protect him. They were very fortunate to gain cover a split-second before the grenade exploded and neither were injured. The citation states: *'Sergeant Seabourne displayed a total disregard of personal danger, and by his courage undoubtedly saved the life of Private Curtis.'*

After the war Dennis Seabourne had several jobs before working for thirty years with the Gas Board at New Inn. He maintained his military connections as a Regimental Sergeant Major with the Griffithstown Territorial Army Battery. Extra to his military duties, Usk Borstal would send him young offenders as a last resort before going to prison. He became known to have a great success rate turning these young lads around. In the years that followed, many of these lads came back to see him and thank him for his support.

A keen gardener in later life, his garden would be admired by many neighbours and he also became an expert fisherman. Quiet moments were spent reading history before this brave and caring man passed away on October 28, 1979, at the age of seventy-two years.

# ARTHUR GEORGE SMITH
## Distinguished Flying Cross

Born 1921, the only son of Mr and Mrs Wilfred Smith, London Terrace, Abersychan, Monmouthshire. Arthur George Smith attended Abersychan Secondary School with his three sisters before joining his father underground at Blaensychan Colliery. As a youth he was a keen supporter of the Boy Scout movement and became a Deputy Scoutmaster in his area before enlisting in 1941.

After joining the Royal Air Force he took part in many operational flights in the Middle East and over Germany. Early in his flying career the young Abersychan man was Mentioned in Dispatches for his good work.

He continued to experience traumatic events and on one occasion his bomber landed in the sea. The Halifax bomber, one of a formation attacking a target in Italy, was on its way home when engine trouble forced the captain to make an emergency landing. The crew of seven took to their rubber dinghy and made for the North African coast, but a strong sea running against them made navigation of the dinghy impossible. After making best use of the small amount of supplies, and later assisted by the people on the shore, they luckily made land after eleven days at sea. His wife, formerly Muriel Stephens, and small daughter, were relieved to hear the good news of his survival.

In July 1945, Warrant Officer A.G. Smith, Royal Air Force Volunteer Reserve, was deservedly awarded the Distinguished Flying Cross.

# GEORGE HEDLEY SMITH
## Mentioned in Dispatches and Distinguished Service Medal

Born 1910, the son of Ada and Frank Smith, 2, North View, Freeholdland, Pontnewynydd, Monmouthshire. Frank Smith worked for many years as a collier at Llanerch Colliery during which time his children, Herman, George Hedley, Garfield and Beryl attended Abersychan School. While in school George showed academic potential which caused the headmaster to take a special interest in him and Miss Cooke, the music teacher, found him a willing pupil.

Leaving school at fifteen years of age George immediately joined the Royal Navy and served in a number of famous warships before transferring to submarines. While based in Scotland, he married Elizabeth Sandford, a young Glasgow lady, on December 28, 1934, and from the happy union two sons was born, Charles Hedley and Colin. The family home would always be in Scotland.

On November 12, 1940, the name of Able Seaman George Hedley Smith, D/JX.126340 appeared in the *London Gazette* for Mention in Dispatches for his good service on the submarine *H.M. Sturgeon*. A few years later, in 1942, he was awarded the Distinguished Service Medal for courage and skill in successful patrols.

Accompanied by his wife, Leading Torpedo Operator G.H. Smith, RN, was invested by the King with the Distinguished Service Medal at Buckingham Palace on Tuesday July 20, 1943.

George Hedley Smith survived the tremendous dangers of a sub-mariner and after serving twenty-six years he retired from the Royal Navy in 1952 to commence employment in Glasgow. Until they went into liquidation he worked for a firm producing optical range finders. This was followed by employment with the giant Hoover Electrical Company, which provided a long and secure occupation until retirement age.

Hedley enjoyed his retirement years. He and his family would often visit his sister Beryl at her Risca home. A keen gardener, he would regularly be seen walking his small Yorkshire terrier. By this time he was an accomplished musician and often entertained with melodious tunes on his piano.

Not many men volunteered for submarine work. The conditions on board were cramped and hot. Even the water was warm to drink. For the safety of his country George Hedley Smith endured all these difficult conditions and showed tremendous courage in the process. This brave man of the sea died in November 1995, age 85 years.

# THOMAS FREDERICK SWEET
### Mentioned in Dispatches

Leading Aircraft Corporal Tom Sweet, RAF, was a quiet man and nothing would change him. His father, F.R. Sweet, while residing at 49a, Brynwern, Pontypool, worked as a telegraph linesman and had won the Military Medal in World War One with the 1st Battalion, the Monmouthshire Regiment. Before joining up Tom was an employee of the Great Western Railway and had been brought up from childhood by his grandmother. He joined the Royal Air Force in 1940, at the age of twenty-three years, and did good work as a bomb aimer during many flights over enemy territory. In 1944 he was Mentioned in Dispatches for, *'cheerfulness and devotion to duty which inspired others to greater efforts.'* He served the remainder of his service attached to the armoury at a bomber base. He was due to go Japan at the end of the war in Europe, but Hiroshima was destroyed and fewer personnel were required.

Returning home after the war he found employment at the Royal Ordnance Factory, Glascoed. He remained in this employment for the rest of his working life. As a young man he enjoyed a game of cricket and later in life became a creditable bowls player. Tom never married and lived with his sister at the family home in Brynwern, Pontypool.

# BERTRAM JAMES THOMAS
### Distinguished Flying Medal

Born 1915, in the Pontypool district, the eldest of three sons of Mr and Mrs Bertram Thomas, of Llantarnam Road, Cwmbran. His education took place at St. Dial's and West Monmouthshire School, where he excelled at music and rugby. His father was well known in the district through his chemist's shop in Commercial Street, Cwmbran. In 1931, at the age of 16 years, he left school to join the Royal Air Force. In October 1940, Flight Sergeant Bertram James Thomas, of Middle East Command, became the proud recipient of the Distinguished Flying Medal.

The weather had been fine when Flight Sergeant Thomas received orders with his flight to dive-bomb an Italian gun position. While over the target, out of the corner of his eye, at the zero minute of attack, he saw an enemy fighter plummeting towards his leader. His bombs shrilled down, and then he raced to his leader's aid. Swiftly the enemy, too, had manoeuvred. There ensued a head-on duel.

If one forgets that the victories of the East were due to sheer skill and heroism, this is a reminder. Out of that duel Bert Thomas emerged with a dreadful wound from an explosive bullet in the right shoulder, and his observer killed. His right arm was useless. Blood was everywhere. He could easily have landed and surrendered to the enemy. Instead he set course for Berbera, the nearest RAF airfield, around forty miles away. Although almost passing out through loss of blood, he made a successful landing with the undercarriage of his aircraft retracted. By his superhuman effort he not only saved his aircraft, but the life of his gunner.

He received his award from King George VI at Buckingham Palace.

During August 1942, Bert was invited back to his old school. At St. Dials School, Cwmbran, he received the gifts of a fountain pen and a book of his own choice, 'Letters of T.E. Lawrence.'

His marriage to Gwen produced a son Peter and daughter Susan. Bert remained in the Royal Air Force until retirement age. His interest in music and rugby continued from his schooldays into his twilight years. This brave man died in 1981 and is buried in Newcastle.

# ALFRED JOHN WADLEY
## Mentioned in Dispatches and Distinguished Service Medal

Born 1913, the eldest son of Mr and Mrs Alfred Wadley, of 48 Oxford Street, Griffithstown, Alf Wadley would win several awards for bravery during World War Two. His father was a shearer in the nearby Panteg Steelworks and, like most lads living in the district, it was expected that Alf would take up the same employment. His education took place at the local school and during holidays he helped out at Bachs', the butchers, Windsor Road, Griffithstown. This led to full time employment at Bachs' until entering the Royal Marines at the age of seventeen years. This career move led to some remarkable adventures. From the very beginning he showed tremendous promise by becoming the proud possessor of the King's badge, for being the best recruit in his squad during the first year of training.

While on leave in December 1937, Alfred John Wadley married Lora Frost, a Newport girl, in her local church. Two sons were born, Alfred John and Michael.

In 1939, he sailed on H.M.S. *Repulse* in which His Majesty King George VI and Queen Elizabeth travelled to Canada, Newfoundland and the United States. It was on the voyage that the King asked Alf if he could borrow his hat, as the royal hat had been mis-laid. He later came into contact with many members of the Royal family, celebrities and film stars, who visited the famous ship when it was in various ports.

Another tour of duty on the *Repulse* in 1939, gave him the opportunity to see Egypt for two years. This was followed by a voyage to the Far East in 1941. By this time the young Griffithstown man had attained the rank of Sergeant Gunnery Instructor. As the ship left Singapore, the captain W.G. Tennant, informed his crew that they were going 'to look for trouble.' They most certainly found it!

On December 10, at 11 o'clock in the morning, Alf was below when he heard a salvo from the ship's guns. At first he thought this was nothing more than a training session. Then the alarm sounded and he quickly grabbed a gasmask and anti-shrapnel helmet before running to his pom-pom gun position. A flight of Japanese bombers approached rapidly. Each in turn dropped their bombs with some resulting in direct hits. Steam pipes burst on the port side of the engine-room, and as the exhaust from the boiler was near Sergeant Wadley's gun position, he was firing in steam from that time onwards.

When Captain Tennant gave the order for all the men to come on deck the message was not heard by Sergeant Wadley and he went on firing. Eventually, Sergeant Wadley left his gun and he found no one left on the ship. A look over the side of the ship indicated a list of seventy-five degrees. The sea was full of thick, black oil. He removed as much of his clothing as possible while looking for a safe place to enter the water. His mind was made up for him when the ship gave a sudden lurch. The next moment he found himself in the water, underneath the ship, and entangled in wire. Although an excellent swimmer, he thought it was the end as everything began to go black. Fortunately, the ship lurched again and set him free. He surfaced and realised that he was badly cut around the body and bleeding profusely from a wound on the head. As best he could, he swam away as the *Repulse* slipped beneath the waves. After half-an-hour he was spotted by a destroyer and brought on board. It was a well-known fact that this part of the sea was shark-infested, but the exploding torpedoes probably frightened them away.

For his gallant action on that black day in British history Sergeant Wadley's name appeared in the *London Gazette*. The citation reads:

> '*The King has been graciously pleased to approve the award of a certificate for Mention in Dispatches for outstanding zeal, patience and cheerfulness, and for setting an example of whole-hearted devotion to duty without which the high tradition of the Royal Navy could not have been upheld.*'

Also carrying out great work against the enemy was his only brother William J. Wadley, who had been in the Royal Air Force since 1936.

After fourteen and a half years Alfred John Wadley was de-mobilised on September 19th 1945 and returned to civilian life. In February 1946, he was pleasantly surprised when a friend showed him the *London Gazette*, which informed that he had been awarded the coveted Distinguished Service Medal. This special award was for gallantry off Norway in 1945, while serving in the cruiser *H.M.S. Devonshire*.

Alf tried several jobs, which included a period working at the Rose Foundry, Newport, before joining the Standard Telephones Company. He stayed with this organisation until he retired thirty-three years later. In his spare time he was skilled photographer and progressed to cine-film when it became popular. Cycling kept him fit until later in life when he developed severe arthritis. To help relieve this crippling illness he emmigrated to Australia to live with his son. He died in Australia ten years later, in 1995.

# MORGAN WATERS
**Military Medal**

Born January 1, 1911, at 35 Grange Road, Lower Pontnewydd, Monmouthshire. His father, Frederick Waters, put food on the table for his large family by working as a collier. With his brothers and sisters Morgan attended St. Dials School, Cwmbran, before joining his father as a collier at Hafodyrynys Colliery. In 1934, a chance meeting led to the marriage of Morgan Waters to Irene May Spanswick, of Pontnewydd. The happy event took place on December 22, 1934, at St. Mary's of the Angels Church, Llantarnam, and a daughter Valerie and son Morgan, were soon to be born. A change of employment saw the young man working at the Royal Ordnance Factory, Glascoed, at the time of enlisting on November 14, 1940.

As a tank commander, he served with the Royal Armoured Corps through the Libyan Campaign and then in Italy. For his work at Normandy on D-Day 3781862 Sergeant Waters was awarded the Military Medal and would later be Mentioned in Dispatches on two occasions for bravery in Germany. His name is to be seen in the January 22, 1946, issue of the *London Gazette*. The account of the action for which he was commended to receive the Military Medal states:

> 'Sergeant Waters, who was a tank gunner throughout the African campaign of 1941 and 1942, and a tank commander in Sicily and Italy, has served as a Tank Sergeant in "B" Squadron since landing on D + 1 until the conclusion of hostilities. He has consistently and uncomplainingly borne the brunt in action after action, and has by his level-headed skill and steadiness in emergency destroyed a disproportionate amount of enemy and their equipment.
>
> 'As a Tank Sergeant of exceptional experience he has repeatedly been called upon to lead the advance in the point tank of his Squadron. Throughout his career no less than seven tanks have been hit and set on fire while he was fighting in them. On each occasion he has quietly and promptly returned to the field in the first available replacement tank. His unwavering, matter-of-fact courage has made him an example, which

*countless of the rank and file have striven to imitate, and he is the type of NCO that is the backbone of a fighting squadron.'*

After the war Morgan worked as a building site foreman for a number of years and later as a popular club steward. Possessing a fine singing voice, he would often be heard giving a solo performance and later in life became a fine gardener. This brave man died on November 8, 1981.

# ARTHUR ALBERT WEBB
**Military Medal**

Born 1915, at Lower Bridge Street, Pontypool, and the son of Lily and Albert John Webb. Arthur's father had served as a Sergeant with the 2nd Monmouthshire Regiment in the First World War and later worked for a while as a collier before becoming a club steward for many years. With his brother and two sisters, Arthur attended Park Terrace School, Pontypool, before taking up employment at Town Forge.

Before the outbreak of war Arthur Webb served in the Territorial Army and responded to his country's call by joining the Rifle Brigade. He went overseas in April 1942, and served in North Africa and Italy with the 8th Army. Always in the thick of the fighting from El Alamein to Tunisia, he was awarded the Military Medal for great personal courage in 1943. The official announcement appeared in the supplement to the *London Gazette*, 22 July 1943. The full citation states:

'*Rifleman Webb was the layer of a six-pounder gun which accompanied the leading Company of 7th Battalion Royal Engineers when the Battalion was ordered to capture the White House, north of Argoubel Regas, on the night of 26/27 April, 1943.*

*After proceeding for 1,000 yards the Battalion came to a narrow defile guarded by six Mk VI German tanks which were protected by at least one Company of German infantry. Under the direction of his Platoon Commander, Rifleman Webb exchanged shot for shot with the Mk VI tanks, hitting them repeatedly at 150 yards range. When his gun received a direct hit, he accompanied his Platoon Commander on two attempts in Bantams to salvage his own gun and one other, both of which had received direct hits. On both occasions the Bantams were set on fire by direct hits when on the point of towing the damaged guns out of the action.*

*Rifleman Webb then dragged his Platoon Commander, who had been rendered unconscious by wounds back to safety and then returned under fire* to try and rescue some more wounded men. *Throughout the action under greatly superior enemy fire at point blank range, he showed great personal courage and devotion to duty.'*

A year later, on Sunday, 30th July 1944, Corporal Arthur Albert Webb, MM., age 29 years, was killed in action in Italy. He was laid to rest at Arezzo War Cemetery, Italy.

On Tuesday April 9, 1946, Arthur's mother, accompanied by her youngest son, Sergeant Horace Webb, of the Green Howards, attended a next-of-kin ceremony at Buckingham Palace to receive from the King, the Military Medal, on behalf of her son.

# JAMES EDWIN WHATLEY
**Mentioned in Dispatches**

Born August 17, 1923, at Cwmbran, Jim Whatley, due to war, became a man destined to have two identities. Like many local men his father earned a weekly wage carrying out the extremely hard, physical work at the Guest, Keen and Nettlefolds iron works, the districts main place of employment. Jim attended the local Catholic School and although not achieving great academic standards, he acquired a rare alertness that would keep him alive through dangerous times later in life. Leaving school at fourteen years of age, he unsuccessfully tried several jobs before enlisting in the 2nd Monmouthshire Regiment several days before his sixteenth birthday. He served until March 1940, but his parents would have none of it and got him out on the grounds of being underage. With the war by then increasing in ferocity, young Jim had already experienced a different and exciting way of life. He became determined to be a part of what he believed to be at the time 'a great adventure'.

Still underage, Jim caught the bus to Newport and at the age of 17 years and 2 months, he joined the British Army under an alias. As James E. Wadley his worried parents never traced him. By the young age of 21 years, through initiative, he wore three stripes on his sleeves. In India he learned the extremely dangerous skill of parachuting and by becoming a signaller, he would always be number one to jump and land before making the all-important messages on his radio.

At the gallant stand by the British and Indian forces during the siege of Imphal, Maiper, a tea plantation area, Sergeant James E. Wadley was Mentioned in Dispatches for his good work against the Japanese. No quarter was given or asked during the Japanese surprise attack. At the critical time his only concern was that the wrong name would be chiselled on his gravestone and relatives would never know what had happened to him. Several enquiries were made by his commanding officer regarding the matter, but to no avail, the British Army would always know him by his alias. While in Germany a Sergeant called "Taff, look at this," the 'Mention' was in Daily Orders, which led to a celebration in the Sergeants' Mess. His citation was published in the *London Gazette* on 27th, September 1945. He spent five years serving on the North-West Frontier and in many other parts of India before going to Burma as a member of the renowned Fourteenth Army. During this time his brother John carried out valuable work in the Merchant Navy.

As James E. Wadley he discharged from the British Army and again became James E. Whatley. He immediately went to New Zealand and tried a number of jobs, while playing the game of rugby in his spare time. Returning home to see his father who was very ill, he would later, in 1954, marry Lily Cole, a Pontnewydd girl. The marriage first took place in a Registry Office and later in Our Lady of the Angels Church, Cwmbran. The happy union brought forth six girls and one boy.

Regular work in the Cwmbran industries provided a well-deserved, comfortable life, which in his younger days would be interrupted for annual visits to his Regiment's reunions.

# ALFRED GEORGE WHEATSTONE
## Military Medal

Born 1919, at the now demolished Hill Street, Pontnewydd. His father worked mainly as a collier and there would be two other sons and five daughters. With his brothers and sisters Alfred George Wheatstone attended the local church school and on completion of his education commenced an apprenticeship with Reynolds, Stonemason, Griffithstown. Before enlisting in the army the young man changed occupations and settled into work at the Cwmbran foundry of Messrs Guest, Keen and Nettlefolds.

By 1944, Corporal Wheatstone, as a member of the 3rd Monmouthshire Regiment attached to the South Wales Borderers, was in the thick of the fighting in North West Europe. On December 19th, 1944, an entry in the *London Gazette* told that No. 3915782 Corporal Alfred George Wheatstone, The South Wales Borderers, had been awarded the coveted Military Medal. The action for which commended states:

> 'On 30th July near St Jean Des Essartiers, when the advance was temporarily held up by German armed cars and a German platoon position, Corporal Wheatstone, after himself being wounded went out single handed with a Bren gun to silence a particular mortar and bazooka position which was causing some casualties. Having finished his Bren magazines, he came back for a Sten gun and ultimately for a rifle and finally silenced the post. It was only after this that he allowed himself to be sent back. His action is worthy of the highest praise and acknowledgement.'

Alfred George, or Sunny, as he preferred to be known, was sent straight to a hospital in Scotland. Recovery was slow and he would always have a disability of the left hand, which he kept covered by a black, leather glove.

Sunny met an attractive, young Cwmbran girl Phyllis Hardwick, and they married at Llantarnam Church in 1948. They had a son William John and two daughters.

Until closure of the Cwmbran branch of Guest, Keen and Nettlefolds in 1956, Sunny worked in their warehouse and would be re-located to their Cardiff works. Later employment at Seaward Jones Engineering, Newport, gave Sunny the opportunity to go to South Africa to help to set up another division of the company.

This local man who showed tremendous courage while enduring great pain, died in August 1987, age 68 years. He is buried at Panteg Cemetery, near Pontypool, Torfaen.

# ALBERT EDWARD WHEELER
### Distinguished Flying Cross

Born in 1911, at Coronation Road, Cwmbran, Albert Edward Wheeler would have a short, but eventful life. His father worked as a furnace man at the nearby Guest, Keen and Nettlefold Iron Works and the future Cwmbran hero had two sisters and two brothers. Early education took place at St. Dial's School and later Abersychan Secondary School. Even as a young lad an aptitude for engineering was very much apparent and he surprised everyone by building a radio that gave out good quality sound programmes.

Leaving school at fifteen years he went straight to RAF Halton and commenced a three-year apprenticeship. He married Doris Potts in 1934, in Chester Cathedral, and two sons were born, John and Robert. Prior to the Second World War he was a Flight Sergeant in a memorable long distance flight staged by the RAF – from England to Australia and back in a Sunderland flying boat. He qualified as a sergeant pilot at the age of twenty-one years and took part in the Battle of Britain and in hunting the *Bismark*.

In July 1941 he was awarded the Distinguished Flying Cross. His citation records:

> '*Since joining the squadron in January 1941, this officer has completed 365 hours operational flying. During a recent period of high pressure, he had a total of 66 hours flying within 7 days. On 5th June, 1941, he was the captain of a Catalina aircraft which carried out a reconnaissance of the Norwegian coast in the Kirkenes and Vadse areas, near the border between Norway and Finland, involving a flight of some 2,500 miles. Despite extremely adverse weather conditions – low cloud and almost continuous snowstorms and visibility as low as 1000 yards – Warrant Officer Wheeler persisted in his mission and made a detailed examination of the area concerned. Although his aircraft was slightly damaged by the fire from an*

*armed merchant vessel, which was encountered after leaving Vadse, Warrant Officer Wheeler flew safely back to his base after a flight of 27 hours. This warrant officer has consistently performed good work and has maintained an unusually high standard of efficiency.'*

His mother and father accompanied him to Buckingham Palace where King George VI presented the medal. His father wished to attend in his Home Guard uniform and there was much upheaval in the Wheeler household finding him a good quality re-placement respirator to complete his apparel for the special occasion.

While acting as an instructor the death took place of Flying Officer Wheeler, DFC, on March 20, 1943. His brother, Jack Wheeler, of Cwmbran, who also did valuable work in the RAF, speaks with fondness of his brother Bert, who did not live to see his two small sons grow up.

# EDMUND VERDUN WILLIAMS
**Mentioned in Dispatches**

Born 1923 and the elder son of William Edmund and Edith Rose Williams, Tan-y-Coed, West Avenue, Freeholdland, Pontnewynydd. His father, who preferred to be known as Ted, was well known in the Pontypool area due to his occupation as a bus driver, with the Western Welsh Company, and a taxi driver. With his brother Sid and sister Mary, Eddie attended Snatchwood School before taking up employment as a lorry driver with W & A. Davies, builders, Abersychan.

In September 1942, at the age of nineteen years, he joined up and became a driver with the Royal Army Service Corps. He landed in North West Europe a week after D-Day and served the remainder of the war abroad until discharging in 1946. It was in 1945 when Driver Edmund Verdun Williams, Royal Army Service Corps, heard that his name had been Mentioned in Dispatches for outstanding good service and devotion to duty with the 21st Army Group. He received a certificate to that effect signed by Field Marshal B.L. Montgomery.

Eddie returned home from Germany and tried a number of driving jobs without success. He seemed happiest when he and his brother Sid commenced a vehicle repair business in a garage near his home in Pontnewynydd. Unfortunately, due to high costs, the venture only lasted a few years. By the spring of 1952, Eddie had met and married Jean Haycox, of Cheltenham. He left the Pontnewynydd district to live at the home of his wife and is said to have lived a long and happy life.

# EDWARD A. C. WILLIAMS
## Croix de Guerre with Palm (Belgian)

Not only would Ted Williams lead a life of compassion, but he was also a very brave young man. Born 1916, in Clifton Place, (now Railway Terrace) Sebastopol, near Pontypool, he attended the village school and Abersychan Technical School. His father, Ernest Edward Williams, worked as a railway employee and served the company for many years as a platelayer. Two more sons made up the family, Frank and Vernon.

Leaving school at fifteen years of age he commenced employment in the nearby Panteg Works Galvanising Department. Aware of how badly the war was going for the British people Ted joined up in 1941 and would later land in Normandy on D-Day.

Ted travelled to the front with the Allied Forces and, with his company, soon became expert at erecting Bailey pontoon bridges, a task so essential for the advance towards Germany. Due to his wide knowledge of first-aid he became a much-needed medic in Belgium and a great support to a Canadian military doctor. On one occasion both men found themselves in the middle of an artillery duel. German and British shells were falling around them. Both men resisted the desire to get to safety and at great danger to themselves, repeatedly removed injured Belgian civilians out of harms way. For their tremendous courage, in 1946, they received the Croix de Guerre from the Belgian Government.

As a Salvation Army member Ted met Vera Dickinson, a pretty young lady from Hull. They married on March 10, 1945, and had a daughter Mavis. For a long time the family lived at Oakland Road, Sebastopol and later moved to Davis Close, Pontypool. Ted did not go back to work in the heavy industry of Panteg Steelworks, but became a railway employee for many years. Later he took up a lighter and more enjoyable employment at Llanfrechfa Hospital, Cwmbran. For many years he would share his hard-earned first aid experience as a dedicated member of St. John's Ambulance Brigade and his life of compassion continued with service to the Salvation Army. Ted passed away on January 29, 1990, age 74 years.

# RICHARD JONES WILLIAMS
## Distinguished Flying Medal

The only son of Mr and Mrs W.D. Williams, 48
Cwmavon Road, Blaenavon. While the
Blaenavon Company employed his father as a
chemist, R.J. Williams was educated at Hillside
School, Blaenavon and West Monmouthshire
School, Pontypool. Prior to the outbreak of war
the young Blaenavon man had been transferred
to the staff of the National Provincial Bank, at
Berkely, Gloucestershire.

During his first tour of operational flights he
took part in the attack on the German
battleship *Tirpitz*. His aircraft was badly hit by
flak on the run in to the *Tirpitz* and the former
Blaenavon airman showed great presence of
mind in extinguishing the fires. Without his
courage the aircraft would have been lost. In
1944, he was awarded the Distinguished Flying Medal.

Flight Sergeant Williams completed a second dangerous tour of operational
flights over enemy territory before the war ended. He returned safely home and
continued his career with the National Provincial Bank.

# HAROLD YOUNG
## Mentioned in Dispatches

Born December 6, 1916, at 39, Rockhill Road, Pontymoile, near Pontypool. Harold Young would undoubtedly have a lifetime passion for the open road. As one of four brothers and six sisters, life was not easy for the lad as he walked the short distance to the nearby Pontymoile Council School. His interest in driving heavy vehicles began early in life and at the very young age of thirteen years, he was already driving lorries around the district during breaks from school. Well built for his age, the boy left school at the age of fourteen years and W. L. Bailey's haulage company had already spotted his rare talent for heavy goods driving. He immediately became a valued employee of the well-known haulage firm.

A keen sportsman, he would regularly be seen on the football field representing the Methodist Church, Pontypool. In 1935, Harold met a girl under the clock of the Pontypool Town Hall and it was love at first sight for the young people. Doris Pearce, from the Race became Harold's wife when they married in the Methodist Church, Pontypool, in 1938.

When realising the seriousness of the war situation Harold Young was in no doubt what he had to do and in May 1940, he enlisted before being trained as a 'fitter' with the Royal Electrical and Mechanical Engineers Corps. Soon, as an experienced worker with heavy goods vehicles, his skill was utilised in a team of three carrying out the work of keeping the roads clear of obstruction. Often under fire, this was vital in the front line of the conflict. Lance-Corporal Young was later pleasantly surprised to be Mentioned in Dispatches and receive the Gold Leaf with the following certificate:

By the KING'S ORDER the name of
Lance-Corporal H. Young,
Royal Electrical & Mechanical Engineers,
was published in the London Gazette on
11 January, 1945,
as mentioned in a Dispatch for distinguished service.
I am charged to record
His Majesty's high appreciation.

P.J. Grigg
Secretary of State for War

Following his discharge in 1945 Harold Young returned to his home at 11 Albion Road, Pontypool, and settled down with his wife and small daughter Patricia. His former job was waiting for him at Bailey's Haulage and he once again became a 'knight of the road.' With the commencement of the New Town, Cwmbran, Harold moved his family to The Lees, West Pontnewydd, where they have lived for over forty years. It was not long before Nationalisation was introduced to the haulage business and Baileys sold out to the British Road Service. Based at Pontymoile, Harold would drive for British Road Service for forty accident free years and be awarded with numerous certificates for his driving skill. He retired from his occupation at 70 years of age and will still be seen carefully driving his car in the Cwmbran area. Married for 65 years, and with four grandchildren and seven great-grandchildren, it is obvious that the open road will always be calling to this brave and resourceful man.